GCSE Computer Science
Non Examined Assessment
Programming Guide

Alan Milosevic, Dorothy Williams

Published by Bagatelle Publications Ltd 2018

Published by Bagatelle Publications Ltd

First published 2018

Printed in the United Kingdom

Set using LaTeX. Serif font 9pt Minion Pro, Sans serif Calibri 9pt.

All source and data files can be downloaded from

`https://github.com/BagatellePublications/GCSE-CompSci-Programming-Guide`

Contents

PseudoCode

Code

Introduction

This guide has been written specifically to help and support those of you currently working on the project section of the GCSE Computer Science qualification. We have taken the three sample scenarios supplied by one of the examination boards, in this case OCR, and one by one have shown how one might approach each of the problems. We have done this from the point of view of an inexperienced student programmer, looking at both what sort of data structures we might use and at what algorithms we might write in order to solve each of the problems.

Each of the solutions is coded in Python. Python comes in two versions, 2.x and 3.x. Because we have intentionally used only those features of the language that every beginning student of Python should be familiar with, the differences between versions are very small. Only the `print` and `input` functions are actually affected - we explain this in on page 4. We could of course have written code to take advantage of more advanced features, many of which might give us a more elegant and more efficient solution. However, a highly efficient, optimised solution isn't what we're aiming for. We are far more interested in showing you how the problem needs to be approached in order to produce a working solution. To help you to understand this, we explain our thinking each step of the way. We suggest how to break the problem down in a sensible fashion, how to write an appropriate collection of functions and we show the type of diagrams and pseudo code we would use. Importantly, we show how to test the code until finally we arrive at a working solution.

This book has been written in a conversational style and the best way of understanding how to approach programming problems is simply to read every word, *especially* the code. If you type the code into Python exactly as and when we do, you'll get a real appreciation of what is going on. After deciding what functions need writing, each function is discussed, expressed in pseudo code and then implemented in the form of a very simple program designed specifically to test the particular function. The final solution to each of the tasks appears over the course of development with the complete code found at the end of each task and also from our website at `https://github.com/BagatellePublications/GCSE-CompSci-Programming-Guide`

After years of teaching students to program, we are only too aware of how difficult it is for many students to get started in programming. Knowing what a particular programming construct such as a *List* or a *for* loop in Python does is one thing but understanding how to use these constructs to produce a working program is quite another. We hope that by showing in detail how we work our way through the thought processes for each of these samples will help you approach the actual task in a more successful manner.

Try not to get discouraged as you work your way through this book; programming is hard. If something we write doesn't seem to make sense, take some time out and come back to it later. Don't try to read the whole book in one sitting. Take your time, think about what we've said. Perhaps you can find a neater way of solving the problem. More than anything else, don't give up. Much like everything in life, the best programmers are those that keep trying no matter how difficult it gets.

1

Useful background information

When we started writing this book, the specification stated that the project represented 20% of your overall mark. You had 20 hours of supervised assessment to complete the project and you had to produce a relatively sophisticated write-up. This has now changed. According to the new guidelines dated the 8th January 2018, you still have to complete one task and all boards are agreed that you shall have 20 hours set aside in the timetable for you to do this. However, the project will no longer be formally marked and consequently, no marks will go towards your final grade.

All examination boards will agree with the above but boards differ with regards to the fine details of the management of the project. Your teacher will know exactly what your board requires.

Many of you will now be wondering what is the point of doing the project if it doesn't count towards your final grade. That's a very good question and for some of you who have absolutely no intention of ever working in any job that requires you to write code of any sort then there is indeed little point. However, the number of jobs available that require no familiarity with code are getting fewer and fewer as time rolls on. These days even the humblest employee is often expected to be able to update a web site. There probably isn't a job in science or engineering that doesn't need some familiarity with code. So unless you really do intend to have nothing whatsoever with computers in the future, tricky when they'll be pretty much running everything, it makes a lot of sense to try to learn how to write some code.

The purpose of this book is to build on what you've been taught by your teachers. We assume that you have some familiarity with Python, but having taught many hundreds of students we are only too aware of how difficult it is to move from knowing about basic ideas like `for` loops and `if then` statements to writing a program.

Our job is to try to take you from knowing some Python to being able to put Python to good use in constructing a program from the ground up. As described in the next chapter, we've taken the three sample tasks that the examination board OCR have written and to help you solve each task you'll need to write pseudo-code, make diagrams of the data structures you're going to use and generally make a bunch of notes. These should be kept, annotated and submitted with your project. As you develop your code, it's extremely important that you test everything that you write - you must show your teacher these tests. We'll show you exactly what we mean as we go through each of these sample tasks. If you follow our thinking carefully for each of the sample tasks hopefully you'll be able to produce a solution for the official task that goes as far as possible in meeting your teacher's expectations.

We've written quite a lot of pseudo code and quite a bit of code. We use a language called LaTeX to write and typeset this book. There are all sorts of stuff in LaTeX that allow us to make the pseudo code look neat and tidy. That's not how it looks when we write things by hand so don't be misled into thinking that your pseudo code has to look anything like ours. The pseudo code package we use automatically adds the `end if`, `end for` and `end while` for us. We only bother adding these when we write by hand if it's necessary to make it clear exactly what code the `if`, `for` and `while` constructs include.

When we transcribe code from our pseudo code we make mistakes just like everyone else. Sometimes the pseudo code is at fault, sometimes we don't code it properly. When things run but don't work properly, we pepper our code with `print` statements and we trace our way through our code carefully to find whatever it is that's causing our code to fail. We test, test and test again. This is part and parcel of development. If we showed you pseudo code that didn't work or code that failed, this book would be many times larger. So don't be fooled. Programming is hard. It takes time and we all fail repeatedly. You probably don't remember learning to ride a bike but I guarantee that you didn't succeed the first, second or probably even the 10th time. Programming is no different.

1.0.1 Annotation

The code that you'll find in this book is very lightly annotated. This is mainly because we've taken some pains to make sure that our variable and function names are self explanatory and shouldn't need much more annotation. In addition, each function that we've written has been preceded by pseudo code and an explanation. We do suggest that when you come to write up your NEA task that in the lines above each function that you write, you include the function name, parameters and return values as in the example below.

```
#------------------------------------------------------------
Function   : winner
Parameters : position (integer)
Returns    : True if position > 48
           : False otherwise
#------------------------------------------------------------
```

2

Python revision

The purpose of this book isn't to teach you how to code in Python; we assume that your teacher has already done this, but we thought that a short chapter on the some aspects of Python that you might not have come across before would help get you started. Firstly though we should give you a little background on the language itself.

2.1 Differences between Python 2.x and Python 3.x

There are currently two versions of Python in common use, Python 2 and Python 3. Most languages move incrementally from one version to another with earlier releases becoming redundant as development moves forward. Python is a little different. Python was originally conceived by a Dutch computer scientist called Guido van Rossum. He remains the central author of the program but of course there are now many, many other programmers involved in the language. He started writing Python in the late 1980s with the first release, version 1.0 arriving in 1994. Version 2.0 appeared in 2000 with versions 2.1, 2.2, 2.3, 2.4 and 2.5 appearing in relatively quick succession.

After 2.5, the developers felt that major design changes to the language were needed that couldn't be implemented by simply changing a few things in version 2.5. They felt that these changes were so large that they couldn't maintain compatibility with the previous versions and decided that a major new release was necessary. In 2008, version 2.5 was upgraded to 2.6 and Python 3.0, the brand new version was created and released. Development pretty much stopped on Python 2 with a final version, Python 2.7 being released simultaneously with Python 3.1 in 2009. Since then Python 2 has had various small changes, mostly cleaning and tidying up existing code but there is no intention to do any further serious development and there will be no version 2.8. Python 2.7 will be supported until at least 2020, with all future development occurring only to Python 3. Releases earlier than 2.7 are no longer supported at all. As of the time of writing, the latest release of Python 2 is 2.7.14 whilst the latest release of Python 3 is 3.6.2.

The small number of differences that are relevant to us affect the use of `input` and `print` statements. Python 2's `raw_input` function is now Python's 3 `input` function. Both functions return a string. In versions of Python 2 prior to but including Python 2.5, `print` is a statement whereas in Python 2.6, 2.7 and 3 it is a function.

The source code in this book has all been written in Python 3 but versions for Python 2 are available at the address given in the Appendix. If you are following our suggestions and are typing the programs into your version of Python, if you have a version earlier than 2.6, you will simply have to change our `input()` functions into `raw_input()` and our `print()` functions into `print` statements. If you are running 2.6 or 2.7 you simply have to change the `input` statements. Note that to find out what version of python you are running you can simply type `python --version` on the command line. Alternatively if you are using IDLE, the very first line that IDLE produces when you start it will tell you the version of Python that you're running.

To explain what we mean, look at the following.

Python 2
`username`= raw_input ("Please enter your username : ")

Python 3
`username`= input ("Please enter your username : ")

Python 2.5 and below
`print` "This is a message"

Python 2.6, 2.7 and 3
`print`("This is a message")

Hopefully this is pretty clear.

2.2 Some basic Python

2.2.1 Types

Python is a strongly typed language. This means that any type that a value has, for example, integer, string, list etc. doesn't change arbitrarily. Integers can't suddenly change into characters or characters into integers. This doesn't mean that the programmer can't change a variable from an integer into a string by re-assigning it, but python itself won't. It is also a dynamically typed language which means that the type is associated at run time.

In order to produce solutions to the three tasks in this book we're going to be concerned with integers, of type `int`, booleans, of type `bool`, strings, of type `str` and lists, of type `list`. Python has a range of other types available including floating point variables of type `float` and dictionaries of type `dict`. These last two aren't necessary for our purposes but they are extremely useful in other circumstances.

Every variable in Python has a type associated with it and the built-in function `type()` will tell you what type your data item has. Take a look at the following session. [Note: user input is indicated in italics]

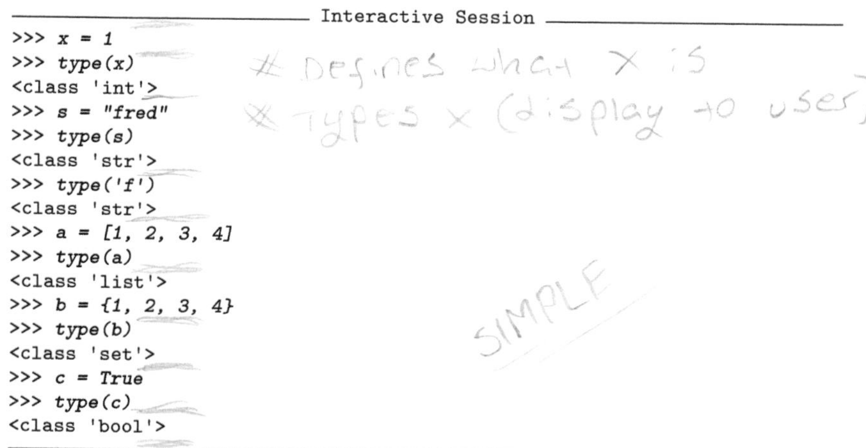

```
Interactive Session
>>> x = 1
>>> type(x)
<class 'int'>
>>> s = "fred"
>>> type(s)
<class 'str'>
>>> type('f')
<class 'str'>
>>> a = [1, 2, 3, 4]
>>> type(a)
<class 'list'>
>>> b = {1, 2, 3, 4}
>>> type(b)
<class 'set'>
>>> c = True
>>> type(c)
<class 'bool'>
```

`x, s, a, b` and `c` are examples of variables. `x` is an `integer`, `s` is a `string`, `a` is a `list`, `b` is a `set` and `c` is a `boolean` which can take on the values `True` and `False`. Whereas in statically typed languages like C, variables are declared to the compiler before being used, in Python this isn't necessary which means that we can simply pluck one 'out of the air' as it were whenever we need one.

But: do remember that each variable is typed - forgetting this is the source of many bugs.

2.2.2 Local and Global Variables

Variables can be *local* or *global*. Local variables are variables that are created and used within a body of code, usually inside a function. They are destroyed as soon as you leave the function. Global variables are variables that can be seen and used inside any function that wants to use them. However to do so, they need to use the keyword `global` as in the following example.

Listing 2.1: Local or Global (testGlobal.py)

```
1  def f():
2    global s
3    print(s)
4    s = "Inside f"
5    print(s)
6
7  # main code starts here
8  s = "Main code area"
9  f()
10 print(s)
```

This produces as output.

Program Output

```
Main code area
Inside f
Inside f
```

So what is happening here? The program starts at line 8 by creating a string variable `s`. Line 9 calls function `f`. In order to 'see' `s` inside function `f` we need to use the keyword `global`. The `print` function on line 3 prints out whatever `s` is currently holding, i.e. `"Main code area"` which is the first thing we see on our screen when the program runs. On line 4 we change what `s` is holding to the string `"Inside f"` which is printed to our screen in line 5. That's the last line in `f` so we leave the function and return to the main code at line 10 which again prints out whatever `s` is now holding. But we changed the value of `s` inside `f`, so what we see printed is not `"Main code area"` which we might have expected to see from looking at the code, but `"Inside f"` instead. Since global variables can be changed by any function anywhere in your code this can lead to bugs which are difficult to track down. Global variables have their place and are often useful, but they can cause confusion and professional programmers avoid them as much as possible.

In contrast, compare this with the following listing where instead of using global variables, we pass `s` as a parameter to `f`.

Listing 2.2: Test Parameter (testParameter.py)

```
def f(s):
  print(s)
  s = "Inside f"
  print(s)

# main code starts here
s = "Main code area"
f(s)
print(s)
```

This produces as output.

```
Program Output
Main code area
Inside f
Main code area
```

The `s` that we pass to the function is copied to a new variable, somewhat confusingly also called `s`, which is then printed on line 2. This `s` is a local variable that will only exist so long as we stay inside `f` and it will be destroyed when we leave. Line 3 changes the value of this local variable `s` to the string `"Inside f"` which is printed on line 4. We leave the function returning to line 8 in the main code where `s` is printed. This `s` has not been modified and we get the result we expect. As a matter of programming style this approach is much preferred and you should write your code to pass and return parameters to and from functions rather than using global variables.

If you're confused, take a look at what is the same code but with the parameter in `f` called `myString` to make the distinction clearer. The output is exactly the same.

Listing 2.3: Test Parameter 2 (testParameter2.py)

```
1 def f(myString):
2   print(myString)
3   s = "Inside f"
4   print(s)
5
6 # main code starts here
7 s = "Main code area"
8 f(s)
9 print(s)
```

If you look at this code closely, it should be clear that the `s` in the main code area is not the same as the `s` that is local to function `f`.

So, in summary

- Don't use global variables unless absolutely necessary (and they rarely are).
- Instead, pass variables into functions as parameters to the function.

2.2.3 Decisions

As with many other languages, you have the opportunity in Python to make decisions. This is achieved using the `if: ...else:` construct as the following example shows.

Listing 2.4: If else (ifElse.py)

```
# if else example

answer = input("What is 3 + 4? ")

if answer == "7":
  print("Correct")
else:
  print("Incorrect")
```

In this snippet, we ask the user for the sum of 3 and 4 hoping to get the answer 7, in which case we'll tell the user that they were correct, else we'll tell them that they were incorrect.

This is pretty clear, but why are we looking for the string consisting of the number `"7"` rather than the number 7 itself?. It's because `input()` in Python 3, or `raw_input()` in Python 2 both return a string **NOT** an integer (this is why understanding what type a variable has is important and in particular understanding exactly what type of variable library functions return). We could easily convert what we get to an integer if we wanted by either wrapping the `input()` function in `int()` as in the following snippet or leaving `input()` alone and then converting it to an integer using `int()` before we test it.

Listing 2.5: If else (ifElse2.py)

```
# if else example

answer = int(input("What is 3 + 4? "))

if answer == 7:
  print("Correct")
else:
  print("Incorrect")
```

We can extend our `if: ...else:` construct indefinitely using `elseif:` as shown in the following snippet.

Listing 2.6: If else (ifElse3.py)

```
# if else example

answer = int(input("What is 3 + 4? "))

if answer == 7:
  print("Correct")
elif answer == 0:
  print("Zero - are you sure")
elif answer == 42:
  print("You've been reading Douglas Adams")
```

```
else:
  print("You're not very good at maths (sigh)")
```

2.2.4 Loops

Python has two main ways for repeating a set of instructions. These are the *while* loop which is a fairly general way of repeating sections of code whilst the *for* loop is designed to allow you to step through items in a particular sequence and to run some code each time. Let's deal with each of these in turn.

2.2.4.1 The while loop

The while loop has the general form

Listing 2.7: General WHILE construct (while.py)

```
while some_condition_is_true:
  do_something
else:
  do_something_else
```

Let's use a `while` loop to print out the numbers 5, 4, 3, 2, 1, 0 in that order. We're going to need to create a variable, say `n` which we'll initialise `n` to 5 by writing `n = 5` **before** we enter the loop. We want to print out each number in turn where each number is 1 less than the previous one. We also want to print out all the numbers including 0. This suggests that we want to keep counting down while the value of `n` is still greater than or equal to zero. Each pass through the loop we'll print the current value of `n` before subtracting one from it. With all of that in mind we end up to with the following piece of code.

Listing 2.8: Counting down (while2.py)

```
n = 5
while n >= 0:
  print(n)
  n = n - 1
else:
  print("BOOM !!")
```

Our output is

Program Output

```
5
4
3
2
1
```

```
0
BOOM !!
```

Break and continue

You might want to break out of a loop before it completes in which case you can use the `break` instruction. When Python sees `break` it'll break out of the enclosing loop (`while` or `for`). The following example shows what we mean.

Listing 2.9: Breaking out (break.py)

```
n = 5
while n >= 0:
  if n == 3:
    print("We're breaking out now!")
    break;
  print(n)
  n = n - 1
else:
  print("Boom !!")
```

The output is

Program Output

```
5
4
We're breaking out now!
```

In this example, we're counting down as before but before we print we check to see whether `n` has reached 3. If we have, we print a message and we immediately exit the loop. Note also that unlike the previous example where we completed the loop we didn't run through the `else` section of the `while` loop. The `else` section runs **only when** we complete the loop. If we break out early, Python will not run the `else` section.

A fairly common example of a `while` is one which starts off with `while True:`. Since `True` is by definition always `True` the only way to leave such a loop is to `break` or to `return` with whatever result we've reached. It's an useful idiom but be careful to ensure that your code can always reach the `break` or `return` statement otherwise your program will never get out of the loop.

2.2.4.2 The for loop

The `for` loop is used extensively to iterate (i.e. repeatedly move) along a sequence of values. The next example shows how to use a `for` loop to count down from 5 to 0. It uses the `range` function to generate a sequence of integers so let's look at `range` before we go any further.

The `range` function

`range` is a very useful function that you will probably use repeatedly. The function takes up to three parameters, each of which must be an integer and in each case produces a `list`.

If only one parameter is given, the value given is the *stop* value and range will generate a set of integers starting from zero and ending at *stop - 1*. For example, `range(5)` generates the `list [0, 1, 2, 3, 4]`.

If two parameters are given, the first represents the *start* value and the second represents the *stop* value. In this instance `range` will generate a `list` of values starting with *start* and ending with *stop - 1*. For example, `range(2, 6)` generates the `list [2, 3, 4, 5]`.

If `range` is given three parameters, the first represents the *start*, the second the *stop* as before whilst the third parameter represents the *step* to be taken. For example, `range(5, 0, -1)` will generate the `list [5, 4, 3, 2, 1]`.

Listing 2.10: Counting down again (for1.py)

```
for n in range(5, 0, -1):
  print(n)

print("Boom !!")
```

which produces the output

Program Output

```
5
4
3
2
1
Boom !!
```

`For` loops can do much more than simply iterate across a range of numbers. Let's suppose that we have a *list* of animals, say `['cat', 'dog', 'pig', 'cow', 'horse']`. (If you've not come across lists before don't worry, we'll take a look at them shortly). We can use a `for` loop to iterate along each one in turn as the following code snippet shows.

Listing 2.11: Printing animals (for2.py)

```
a = ['cat', 'dog', 'pig', 'cow', 'horse']

for animal in a:
  print(animal)
```

This little piece of code will produce the output

```
Program Output
cat
dog
pig
cow
horse
```

Here, the **for** loop is working it's way along the list pulling out each of the items one at a time and giving them to us to do something with. In this case we simply print whatever we're given but as you'll see when we come to produce code for each of the three projects we can do much more complex things with each of the items.

2.2.5 Strings

You're almost certainly familiar with using strings in Python so we won't spend too much time discussing them here apart from pointing out a few things that you might not have come across.

For example, if you have created a variable called `myString` and initialised it to *"My test string"*, searching for "str" by using the `find()` method will give you the index of the start of "str". You can split the string into it's individual words by using the method `split()` and you can see how long the string is by typing `len(myString)`, all of which are shown below.

```
Interactive Session
>>> myString = "My test string"
>>> len(myString)
14
>>> myString.find('str')
8
>>> words = myString.split()
>>> words
['My', 'test', 'string']
>>> words[0]
'My'
>>> words[2]
'string'
```

Having split `myString` into the individual words, now stored in `words`, we can now print out each of the individual words by simply using a `for` loop as in the following code snippet.

Listing 2.12: Extracting words from a string (words.py)

```
myString = "My test string"

words = myString.split()

for word in words:
  print(word)
```

Our output is

Program Output

```
My
test
string
```

If you're wondering what sort of thing `words` is, you'll find by typing `type(words)` that it's a `list` which means that there are all sorts of things that ywe'll be able to do with it as we'll show later.

Slicing

Taking `myString` as our example, take a look at the following interactive session with Python.

Interactive Session

```
>>> myString
'My test string'
>>> myString[0:12]
'My test stri'
>>> myString[8:-2]
'stri'
>>> myString[4:7]
'est'
>>> myString[-6:-1]
'strin'
>>> myString[-6:]
'string'
```

Remember that Python indexing starts at 0, so in the first case `myString[0:12]`, we've asking Python to extract characters from `myString` from position 0, i.e. the start , up to but not including position 12. `myString[8:-2]` asks Python to extract the string starting at position 8 and ending 2 positions from the end of the string, essentially removing the last two characters of the string. `myString[4:7]` asks Python to take out a slice of the string starting at position 4 and ending (but not including), position 7. This slice removes three characters. `myString[-6:-1]` asks Python to take a slice starting 6 characters from the end of the string and ending at the character that's 1 position before the end of the string. The final example `myString[-6:]` asks Python to take a slice starting six characters from the end up to the end of the string.

The following diagram should make this clear.

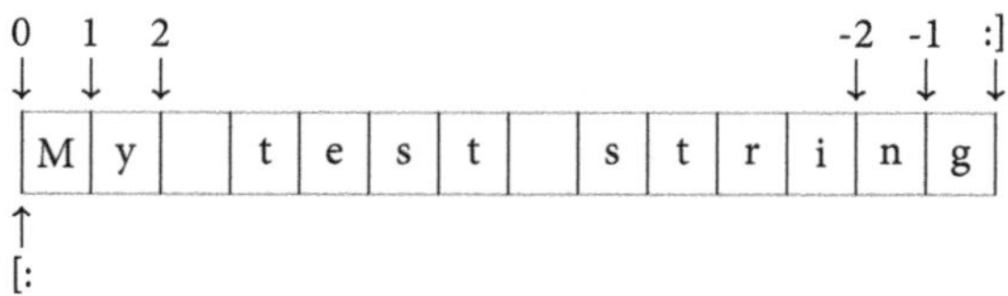

Printing strings

One useful debugging technique is to insert `print` statements in amongst your code. The `print` statement is very versatile and one useful feature is best explained with an example.

Let's suppose that you want to print out a message which includes whatever is in the variable `myString` and also shows you how long it is. Using `print` you could do the following.

```
print ("Mystring is '%s' and it is %s characters long" % (myString,
len(myString)))
```

which gives the following as output.

```
Mystring is 'My test string' and it is 14 characters long
```

Whenever `print` sees '%s' inside a string that it's about to print it will replace it with whatever it finds at the appropriate place in the brackets that follow the closing quotes and final % symbol. The first '%s' it sees gets replaced with the first item it finds, in this case `myString`. The second '%s' is replaced with the second item, i.e. `len(myString)` which in our case is 14.

Converting strings to numbers and vice versa

Often we need to convert numbers to a string and a string to a number. `str` will convert any number, integer or floating point to a string, whereas `int()` and `float()` will convert a string of the right format into an integer and a float respectively.

e.g.

Interactive Session

```
>>> number = 4.56785
>>> str(number)
```

```
'4.56785'
>>> s = '3.142'
>>> float(s)
3.142
>>> number = 1239
>>> str(number)
'1239'
>>> s = '414332'
>>> int(s)
414332
```

2.2.6 Lists

Lists are really useful. They're an example of a *collection*. They contain other objects of all sorts of types. A list L for example might contain some numbers, strings and possibly another list.

```
L = [3.14159, "Frederick", 12, [14, 23, "Thompson"], True]
```

This first item in this list is clearly a floating point number, the second is a string, the third an integer, the fourth is another list whilst the last item is a boolean, in this case `True`. The enclosed list contains three elements, two integers and a string, `Thompson`. Let's look at how we can access each of the elements in L. Do read through each of the lines carefully and make sure that you understand exactly why Python responds in the way that it does.

Interactive Session

```
>>> L = [3.14159, "Frederick", 12, [14, 23, "Thompson"], True]
>>> len(L)
5
>>> L[0]
3.14159
>>> L[1]
'Frederick'
>>> L[2]
12
>>> L[3]
[14, 23, "Thompson"]
>>> L[4]
True
>>> len(L[3])
3
>>> L[3][0]
14
>>> L[3][1]
23
```

```
>>> L[3][2]
'Thompson'
>>> L[3][2][0:4]
'Thom'
>>> L[0][1]
Traceback (most recent call list):
  File "<stdin>", line 1, in <module>
TypeError: 'float' object is not subscriptable
>>> len(L[1])
9
>>> L[1][0]
'F'
>>> L[1][2:4]
'ed'
```

Hopefully all of the above will make sense to you. Because L[1] is the string `Frederick', it's possible to use a second subscript to pick out any or all of the letters of `Frederick'. Similarly, because L[3] is itself a string, using a second subscript will allow us to get to each of the elements. Indeed, because the third and last element of L[3] is a string, i.e. `Thompson', we can get to the individual letters in `Thompson' using a third subscript as shown in the example. Notice that when we try to use an additional subscript on L[0] which is a floating point number, we get an error message because it's not possible to access any of the individual numbers inside the float.

Now that we're clear on how to get to any individual element of a list, let's look at how we might use a **for** loop to print out the relevant information.

Listing 2.13: Printing items from a list (lists.py)

```
L = [3.14159, "Frederick", 12, [14, 23, "Thompson"], True]

print('Our list L holds the following items')
for item in L:
  print(item)

print("The second item (a string) consists of the following characters")
for item in L[1]:
  print(item)

print("The list inside L holds the following items")
for item in L[3]:
  print(item)
```

This short piece of code generates the following output.

Program Output

```
Our list L holds the following items
3.14159
```

```
Frederick
12
[14, 23, 'Thompson']
True
The second item (a string) consists of the following characters
F
r
e
d
e
r
i
c
k
The list inside L holds the following items
14
23
Thompson
```

In the three example coursework pieces set by OCR we'll need to make extensive use of lists so please make sure that you understand everything that we've covered here.

3

The tasks

In this book we have used three tasks provided by the examination board, OCR, that are intended to give you an idea as to the sort of problem that you might expect to be given for the final assessment. Many schools no doubt use them as practise tasks in preparation for writing the official task when it becomes available towards the end of the course. Your teacher will be given three official tasks from which you must complete one. Some teachers allow their students to make their own choice. Others, probably the majority, will insist that everyone completes the same task. Allowing you to choose sounds good in principle but it's harder for the teacher to keep track of, it can make it more difficult for the teacher to provide the appropriate help and support and the benefit to you is often more perceived than real. Additionally, although all three tasks should be of the same difficulty, in practice, depending on what you have learned throughout the year, some tasks might be easier than others. As a final comment, some tasks are more easily programmed in some languages than in others. All of this your teacher will know when making their decision.

With that said, if the teacher does give you the opportunity to choose your own task be very careful in your choice, as it will be difficult if not impossible to change it if you get into difficulty.

3.1 The sample tasks

The three sample tasks that OCR have produced vary quite a bit in difficulty. The first task asks you to build a simple collection of data, i.e. a very small database that you need to add data to, query and produce three simple reports. This is an ideal task for Python, the user interface is simple and Python has all of the language constructs and data objects necessary to tackle this sort of task quite easily. We show you how to approach this problem and we also guide you through producing the sort of well-tested code that your teacher wants to see. We strongly suggest that you read through this sample task very carefully. All of the code is on our website but you really should enter the code line by line as you read along with us. You might think that you'd learn quicker by reading the text, downloading and running the code but you'd be wrong. You'll learn quicker and more thoroughly by actually typing in the code. Doing so forces you to read the code carefully. You'll probably make mistakes entering the data. Surprisingly, making mistakes is a good thing - you'll learn a lot by finding and fixing your errors.

The second task requires you to write a program to suggest films to watch based on films that you've liked in the past. To produce a proper working program you'll really need to construct a small (> 25) collection of films and customer details in order to test the code properly. We've done this for you and the data is listed in the appendix but is also on our web site. In this instance we do suggest that you download the data files rather than typing them in yourself though it is important to take a careful look at the data. The data structures that you need to use are trickier than you might have been used to. You'll need to construct a list which has lists as elements and in the case of films that you've watched, the last element is itself a list of lists. This isn't necessarily difficult but you may not have spent much time looking at nested lists and most likely you've not come across nested lists of nested lists before. We've tried to explain how to approach this sort of problem in quite some detail but don't be too alarmed if you find it difficult; the other two samples are much more straightforward.

The third task asks you to write a game, essentially snakes and ladders for two players. It's unclear as to whether you're being asked to roll a couple of physical dice but as you'll see it's much quicker to develop the code on the assumption that you're running a simulation of two dice. Writing it as a simulation will allow you to test the code very much faster than playing it with physical dice. Each run through the simulation will take a few milliseconds and you can get it to produce a full listing of what's happened on each run. Once you know that the game is working correctly you can switch to physical dice, which simply means changing a couple of lines of code. The game is to take place on a 7 x 7 grid but as you'll see as we develop the code, it's not necessary and in fact it's actually a distraction to worry about the grid while you're developing the gameplay code. Once the gameplay is complete and fully working, it's very straightforward to add the graphical element where the job of the grid is simply to display the position of the two players.

We're assuming that your Python programming is reasonably good and in the previous chapter we introduced you to a small number of slightly more advanced ideas. In our explanation of how to approach each of the tasks, we've tried to explain any more advanced language construction as we go along. We assume that you're familiar with `if` and `while` statements and that you're comfortable with `for` loops. As we mentioned earlier, it's good programming style to avoid global variables as much as possible and you'll see that we pass parameters into functions and return values back again rather than use a global variable. We've tried to choose sensible variable and function names throughout and although Python doesn't have constants as such, when a variable is not intended to change we've written it in capital letters, e.g. SIMLULATION or BOX_X and we've explained exactly what they mean. We've added comments where necessary, this is called annotation and while it's a very important part of programming, if you use good variable and function names, you'll find that the number of comments that you need to have in your code will actually be surprisingly small. The best written code is essentially self-documenting.

We've stressed throughout the importance of testing. Almost all of the listings in this book are fully working little programs designed to test one thing. When you produce your final write-up it's critical that you show your teacher that you have tested your program as thoroughly as you can. There are so many ways for programs to fail. There are sophisticated techniques employed by professional programmers in certain situations that can to some extent verify that a program does what it is supposed to do, but these situations are few and far between so testing, testing and more testing is the order of the day. No amount of testing will ever guarantee that a program is bug free, but extensive testing will remove many of the more obvious bugs.

We've tried to lead you through the code as carefully and as clearly as we can but everyone thinks and works in different ways. Hopefully by scrutinising our text and code very closely, what we are doing and more importantly, why we are doing it will become clear. Don't try to rush through each of the tasks. Take your time and think hard about what and why we are approaching the problem in the way that we do. There are many ways to tackle a problem and there are always alternative ways of writing code - that's part of the enjoyment of programming. Our code seems to us to be relatively clear and straightforward, hopefully you will agree.

3.2 Language choice

This particular edition uses Python to solve these three tasks. However, most of the this book is about how to think and what to do using pencil and paper. We turn to coding only after we've worked out exactly what we need and why we need it. It's important to be familiar with Python in order to write the actual code, but the clearer you are in your thinking about the problem, the simpler it will be to code. Hopefully all of this this will become apparent as you work your way through the book.

As we discussed earlier, Python comes in two main flavours - Python 2.x and Python 3.x. The code in this book will run exactly as is if you are using verions 3.x. The differences between Python 2 and Python 3 only affect `print` and `input` which means that with only very small changes anyone who is limited to Python 2 should have no difficulty getting this code to run. In any case, the code on our website is available in both versions.

In each of the tasks we make use of external libraries. Where we do so we simply `import library` rather than using the Python command `from library import *`. In the first case we'll need to precede every use of a function from the library with library name followed by a dot. This necessitates some extra typing but the advantage of this approach is that it makes it explicit that the function comes from the external library and is not part of standard Python. It also means that if one inadvertently creates a function with the same name as a function in the library, because the library function's full name includes the name of the library, there is no name clash and both can co-exist.

3.3 Debugging

Nobody, and we really do mean nobody, writes programs larger than a few lines of code that work first time. All programs have bugs[1] in them. Yours will too. Wikipedia defines a bug as an *error, flaw, failure or fault in a computer program or system that causes it to produce an incorrect or unexpected result, or to behave in unintended ways*[2]. Getting rid of bugs is achieved by testing, testing and yet more testing. Professional programmers often adopt what is called a *test driven* methodology where tests are written before the code that's going to be tested. This might sound silly, but it's a very effective way of focussing the programmer's mind on what is important before writing any code.

In this approach, programs are divided into very small pieces of functionality and a test is written. It runs, it fails (because at this point the programmer hasn't actually written any code to solve the problem) and then the programmer writes code to ensure that the test passes. When it does he or she moves on to the next small piece. The process continues until the program is finished. Importantly, every time the developing program is tested, ALL the tests are rerun. This ensures that while the programmer is developing a new part of the project that might possibly modify some earlier code, anything that has been broken will be picked up immediately by the tests.

We're not going to follow that methodology to the letter in this project, but we will break the problem down into small pieces and we will test every piece independently before stitching everything together and testing the whole program. It's important when testing that you have a very clear picture of exactly what is going on whilst the program is running. This usually means needing to know exactly what is happening to your variables and data structures. Putting lots of `print` statements into your code is one way. Writing small *helper* functions to load example data and to display variables and data structures on demand is another complementary way. To show you what we mean, one of the first pieces of code that we'll write will be to create an example data file. We'll write a function to load the data file and another function to show the data structure that we're going to use internally to hold our data.

You'll make mistakes and introduce bugs all of the time when you're coding. You'll reduce the number as you become more experienced; you'll reduce them quicker if you type carefully. Most of all, you'll need to be patient, you must not get upset when your program doesn't work. Instead, you should introduce a few `print` statements, run the code again, see what your print statements show you, think, change your code and run it again.

3.4 Programming Style

Before we start it's worth making a few comments regarding programming style. Every programmer develops his or her own style of programming. This covers how they think,

[1] `https://thenextweb.com/shareables/2013/09/18/the-very-first-computer-bug/#.tnw_UEJu38eh`

[2] `https://en.wikipedia.org/wiki/Software_bug`

how they break problems apart, how they write and how they debug code. People who program for a living often have to follow particular guidelines laid down by the organisation they work for. This will cover how they document their code, how they name their variables and functions and how their code should interact with their colleagues.

You might think that programmers working alone could do pretty much what they please, but you'd be wrong. Lone programmers are actually always working alongside someone else - their future selves, who take less than kindly with being handed unintelligible code to debug and maintain later. As a programmer you owe it to yourself to document your code thoroughly, to keep paper copies of your notes and algorithms that you produced during development. If you choose your variables and function names wisely your code will need little additional annotation. Test thoroughly and frequently. Every function should be tested exhaustively before being added to the growing body of code. If you have an advanced IDE (Integrated Development Environment) you'll be able to step through your code, insert breakpoints and monitor the values of your variables whenever you want. If you don't have such tools to play with, put lots of `print` statements inside your code so that you can see when you enter and exit functions, modify variables and exit loops.

We are somewhat old fashioned and use an editor called `vi` and the command line to write and run our code and in order to keep this book to a reasonable size, we've omitted all of the print statements that we insert routinely when we write code. The code you'll find here and on our web site is code that works, not because we're astonishingly brilliant programmers but because we're not showing you the code that didn't work and needed to be debugged thoroughly before we finally removed the `print` statements that we liberally littered around.

The most important characteristic of a good programmer is persistence, i.e. not giving up.

GOOD LUCK.

4

Sample Task 1

Scenario

When new students arrive at Tree Road School, they are assigned:

- a unique ID number
- a tutor group
- a unique school email address

A tutor group contains approximately 25 male and female students.

Mr Leeman is a form tutor and wants a simple computer system to manage his tutor group.

Mr Leeman wants to be able to have a user friendly interface that allows him to log into the system and carry out the necessary administration.

The details of the students that Mr Leeman needs are:

- unique ID number
- surname
- forename
- date of birth
- home address
- home phone number
- gender
- tutor group
- unique school email address.

Analyse the requirements for this system and design, develop, test and evaluate a program that allows Mr Leeman to:

1. log in with a username and password
2. access a menu system
3. enter and store the students details
4. log out

5. retrieve and display the details of any student when Mr Leeman enters the student's unique ID number.*
6. create at least three different reports that Mr Leeman might need, and describe how he would use each one.
7. produce these reports when selected from a menu.

*Note for candidates:
In order to test this program, you will need a data file containing the details of at least 25 students.

So, where do we start?

Reading the text carefully we can see that we need to keep track of up to 25 students, each of which has some information associated with them - unique ID number, surname, forename and so on. We've also got to allow Mr Leeman to log in and out, access a menu system to enter and store student information, produce at least three different reports and retrieve information on a student given their unique ID number.

The user interface needs to be friendly, hence the menu system.

The first thing you should do is to try to imagine what we call the life cycle of the program.

4.1 Life Cycle

Mr Leeman will start the program, by typing something like `python myProgram.py`. The program will start and the first thing it should do is to ask him to log in, asking him for a username and password. If the username matches, he'll be asked for his password and if that matches the one that we've got for him he'll see the main menu system that will allow him to carry out the rest of the tasks - entering student information etc. One of the menu options should allow him to log out. When he does, the program will stop.

At this point we should draw a simple picture of the life cycle showing the important points. When you're writing up your project you should keep all of your drawings and notes and either submit them as part of the project or prettify them by using a software tool such as *Dia Diagram Editor*[3] which can produce drawings very similar to the one in figure 4.1.

Figure 4.1: Life Cycle

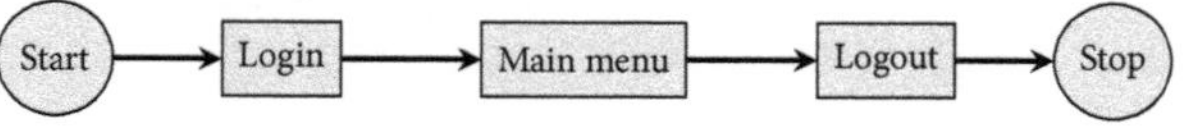

[3]https://sourceforge.net/projects/dia-installer/files/latest/download

The approach we're taking here is called top-down design, also called stepwise refinement. We start out by breaking down the problem in as simple a fashion as we can. We can't really make it much simpler than the diagram in Figure 4.1. Mr Leeman is going to start the program, he'll login, use the main menu, logout and the program will stop. Later we'll need to draw diagrams of each of these stages in more detail and then perhaps even take those diagrams and break them down further. Eventually, once we have a really clear picture of exactly what we're doing we'll start writing some code.

Let's start with the login function.

4.2 Login

The job of the login function is to check that Mr Leeman has entered his username and password correctly. We'll ask him to enter his username and if it matches, we'll ask for the password and if that also matches we'll carry on with the program, but if it doesn't there's really no point in continuing so we should stop the program with an error message.

This suggests that the pseudo code for the login process would look something like this.

PseudoCode 4.1 Login

```
procedure LOGIN
    ask for the username
    if the username matches the one we have then
        ask for the password
        if the password matches the one we have then
            return True
        end if
    end if

    return False
end procedure
```

This is pretty straightforward so we can go ahead and write some code for this immediately. It's very self-contained and should be put into its own function. We're going to make a decision to proceed based on whether Mr Leeman has entered his username and password correctly so the function should pass back to us the value `True` if he did and `False` if he didn't. In the main body of the program where we call this function we'll continue if we got `True` and stop with an error message if we didn't.

What shall we call this function?

If we could simply write this in plain English, we'd probably say something like *If the login was successful do A else do B*. Given that in code we'll actually write something pretty close to this, a good name for the function might be `loginWasSuccessful()`. In which case the main code will look like this.

```
if (loginwasSuccessful()):
  tell the user that login was successful
else:
  tell the user that login failed
```

Choosing good names for functions and variables is really important, it helps make your program self-documenting and easy to read.

The next question that arises however is where shall we hold Mr Leeman's username and password. We're going to compare what he gives us with what we've got stored, so where should these two pieces of information be stored? We could keep them in plain text in the program. We could make the login process a little more secure from prying eyes by keeping the username and password in a file that's stored on the hard disk. We could do all manner of clever things if we really put our mind to it and if we were asked to do this sort of thing for a commercial program we'd also really need to keep at least the password encrypted. But, because this is a school project, let's keep it really simple and store both username and password in plain text in the program itself in which case the following code will do the job nicely.

Listing 4.1: Simple login (loginSimple.py)

```
MR_LEEMANS_USERNAME = 'pleeman'
MR_LEEMANS_PASSWORD = 'abcd1234'

def loginWasSuccessful():
   username = input("Hello, please enter your username: ")
   if username == MR_LEEMANS_USERNAME:
      password = input("Hello Mr. Leeman, please enter your password: ")
      if password == MR_LEEMANS_PASSWORD:
         return True

   return False

# main program starts here
if loginWasSuccessful():
   print("Correct username and password")
else:
   print("Incorrect username or password")
```

Since we're only concerned at the moment with the login function, we won't bother including code to do anything other than this one task.

Note that although Python doesn't officially have constants, we've followed the usual conventions and put what we consider to be constant values into the all capital letter variables MR_LEEMANS_USERNAME and MR_LEEMANS_PASSWORD.

Run this program and check that the programs prints the correct message when the username and password are both entered correctly. If the username is incorrect the code won't bother asking for the password. If the username is correct it'll ask for the password and then pass back **True** if it matches. If either is incorrect it'll pass back **False** with the message `Incorrect username or password' as shown below.

Program Output

```
Hello, please enter your username: askajhd
Incorrect username or password
```

Program Output

```
Hello, please enter your username: pleeman
Hello Mr. Leeman, please enter your password: abasd323
Incorrect username or password
```

Program Output

```
Hello, please enter your username: pleeman
Hello Mr. Leeman, please enter your password: abcd1234
Correct username and password
```

This works fine but in the real world most people are given more than one attempt to enter their password before the program gives up. We can't let him try indefinitely but we could allow him a small number of attempts before calling it a day and returning **False** to the main body of code.

Let's give Mr Leeman three attempts.

If he's still not got it right after three attempts then we'll give up and return **False**. If on the other hand he does on one of the three attempts get the password correct, then we'll pass back **True** to the main body of code and we can then continue with his admin stuff.

So, what does the logic look like?

- We're going to have to loop around waiting for him to get the right password.
- We're going to have to keep track of the number of attempts that he's made.
- If he's had three we'll leave the function and return a value of **False**.

We'll start some sort of counter to keep track. We'll start it off with the value 0 and we'll add one to it every time he makes an attempt. We could write this as a flow chart, but pseudo code, shown below works just as well if not better.

PseudoCode 4.2 Login was successful

```
procedure LOGIN WAS SUCCESSFUL
    Ask for the username
    if the username is correct then
        Set counter = 0
        while counter < 3 do
            Ask for the password
            if the password is correct then
                return True
            else
                counter = counter + 1
            end if
        end while
    end if

    return false
end procedure
```

Listing 4.2 shows how we might code it. Notice how similar it is to the pseudo code.

Listing 4.2: Login with counter (loginWithCounter.py)

```python
MR_LEEMANS_USERNAME = 'pleeman'
MR_LEEMANS_PASSWORD = 'abcd1234'

def loginWasSuccessful():
    username = input("Hello, please enter your username: ")
    if username == MR_LEEMANS_USERNAME:
        counter = 0
        while counter < 3:
            password = input("Hello Mr. Leeman, please enter your password: ")
            if password == MR_LEEMANS_PASSWORD:
                return True
            else:
                counter = counter + 1

    return False

# main program starts here
if loginWasSuccessful():
    print("Correct username and password")
else:
    print("Incorrect username or password")
```

In this listing we start by asking for the username. If the username matches we set `counter = 0`. We then enter and remain inside a `while` loop until `counter` has reached the value 3 or he enters the password correctly. Inside the loop we ask Mr Leeman for his password. If it's correct we exit the function immediately and return `True`. If he fails, we add 1 to `counter`, we go back to line 8 and check again whether `counter < 3`. If it is, he gets another go. If not, we don't enter the loop but instead drop to line 15 and return `False`. Depending on what is returned, the main body of the program can then either issue a sensible goodbye message or continue.

That's the login section completed. At this point you need to run this program and test it with a variety of passwords, checking that the code works exactly as required. Once you've done this - and fully documented that you have indeed tested it properly we can carry on to look at the administration that Mr Leeman wants to carry out.

4.3 Student Data Structure

It's time now to move on to the heart of the project. Mr Leeman wants to enter new student information, he wants to search for a student using their unique ID and he wants to create three different reports. For each student, he wants to keep track of their *unique ID, surname, forename, date of birth, home address, home phone number, gender, tutor group* and *unique school address.* This represents 9 pieces of data for every student. The scenario points out that to test the program properly we'd need to keep track of at least 25 students.

In database terminology, the pieces of data that we're going to store for every student are called *fields* and each student represents a single *record.* So, we need to keep at least 25 records where each record has exactly 9 fields. If this were a larger program we'd consider using a database but this is a small school project. Since Python has perfectly good data structures for holding and manipulating this sort of information there's no need to go to the time and effort of installing, setting up and using a database.

So let's start with the data. Eventually we are going to hold 25+ records, each of which has exactly 9 fields. The simplest Python data structure for holding a record is a `list`. Python has excellent functions for dealing with `lists` so using a single `list` for a single student makes sense. What about 25 or more students? Python `lists` can hold pretty much anything, including other `lists`. So logically, our collection of records would be a `list` of `lists`.

Before we go any further, let's make this concrete by creating an example of what we're intending to keep. Each student `list` has to hold 9 fields so let's make up some student data holding all of the fields that we need to see in exactly the form that Python will use.

Suppose that Tree Road School has a student called *Peter Parker*, with a unique ID of `23876`, a unique school email address of `23876@treeroad.sch.uk`, a date of birth of `23-05-2003`, a home address of `"34 Parkway, Marston, Oxford, OX2 OUD"`, a home phone number of `01865325645`, he is male `M` and is in tutor group `5LM`. If we follow the same order as the scenario has given us, we'd construct a `list` with the following contents:

```
[23876, Parker, Peter, 23-05-2003, "34 Parkway,Marston, Oxford,
OX2 OUD", 01865325645, M, 5LM, 23876@treeroad.sch.uk]
```

Notice that we have exactly 9 fields. Python starts counting from 0, so our first field, i.e. the one holding the unique ID has an index of 0. The second field which holds the surname has index 1, the third holding his forename has index 2 and so on until the 9th field, with index 8 which holds the unique email address. If we construct a `list` holding information on Tim Tomas as well we'll construct a Python `list` data structure each of whose elements are `lists`. In this case it would like like this …

```
[
[23876, Parker, Peter, 23-05-2003, "34 Parkway, Marston, Oxford,
OX2 OUD", 01865325645, M, 5LM, 23876@treeroad.sch.uk],
[17893, Tomas, Tim, 12-06-2003, "15 The Oaks, Marston, Oxford,
OX2 OTY", 01865112233, M, 5LM, 17893@treeroad.sch.uk]
]
```

We've deliberately laid this out with opening and closing square brackets on separate lines to highlight the fact that we have a `list` data structure holding two `lists` as data elements.

This can be extended indefinitely allowing us to hold as many students as we want. For what's coming next we need something to call our `list` of 25+ students. For fairly obvious reasons let's call it our `studentList`.

One of the things that the project scenario wants us to write code for is to enter new student information. If we've already got data in an existing `studentList` we simply need to `append` a new single `list` of student information to the `studentList`. If this were our first student, we'd simply create an empty `studentList` and `append` the new student list to it.

We also need to write some code to search for a unique ID. This simply means that we need to read `studentList` and search the first field in every element (each of which is a `list` holding information on a single student) in `studentList` for the unique ID that we're looking for.

We've also been asked to write code to create three reports from the data. An example of a report might very well be to produce a display of all the boys in the tutor group. In which case we'll simply look at the 6th field, i.e. the gender field, in each element (i.e. student) in `studentList` and display the name when we find an `'M'` in that field.

It seems therefore that pretty much everything that we've been asked to do on this task revolves around `studentList`. Consequently, as you'll see shortly, most of the code that we write from now on will either do something with or do something to our `studentList`.

In order to test the code that we're going to write, we're going to need examples of student information. We could write the code to enter new information first and then run that function every time that we need to test the other functions that we need to write such as searching and producing reports. This will prove to be very tedious and there is a much better way. It'll take a little time and effort but if we used a text editor to create a simple text file of say 26 students with all of the fields filled in, this will save us hours of repeatedly entering data. We can save this example file on our hard disk and load it at the start of any program that we write. We'll pull the data directly into a brand new `studentList` data structure and then we can play with this to our heart's content. Since this data structure is so important, we will also write a function to display the contents of this data structure whenever we want.

Python has simple functions to read and store lines of text, so now is the time to either get out your text editor and create 26 students with all of their details or alternatively download our example data file from our web site. (We've printed a copy of the file in the Appendix). We've saved our students in a datafile called `students.csv` which is used throughout the rest of this chapter. The format that we've adopted is known as a *comma separated* file format, most commonly called `csv`. A `csv` file is simply a text file where each item on a line is separated by a comma. We've created 26 students so the file will have 26 lines with each line holding nine fields separated by commas. Since the address field might very well have commas in it we don't want to confuse python so we'll enclose the address field in quotation marks, thus hiding these commas. The remaining fields don't need them.

Python has a library dedicated to loading and saving data in this format. It's called `csv` and has a number of functions dedicated to reading and writing `csv` files. Since we're currently concentrating on loading data from the file, the only function we're interested in at the moment is the `reader` function which reads a line of input and stores it in a `list`.

If you look very carefully at the full set of students, you'll see that we've deliberately left out some data and some are obviously incorrect. For example, `May Priest` has her birthday on `11-11-2102`, the telephone number for `Megan Hignam` has 12 digits and `Hannah Gras` hasn't been given a home address. Missing and erroneous data is inevitable when real life data is put into a computer system so we've mimicked that here. We've still not finally decided what reports we want to allow Mr Leeman to create - perhaps a useful one would be to show him which students have missing telephone numbers or addresses for example.

Before we do anything else let's write two functions. The first we'll call `loadStudentData` whose job it will be to try to load the student data off the hard disk. If it succeeds it should pass the new list back to us. If it fails it should tell us and return an empty list to prove it. The second function we'll call `displayList(L)` which will print on the screen the contents of whatever list `L` we give it. You'll soon see that these two functions are in many ways the most important that we'll write. With them in place, writing and more importantly, testing everything else will be made much, much easier.

The pseudo code for our first function, `loadStudentData` will look something like this.

PseudoCode 4.3 Load student data

```
procedure LOAD STUDENT DATA
    try to open the student data file
    if this fails then
        print "Failed to open file"
        return an empty list to show that nothing was loaded
    else
        print "File was opened successfully"
        load the student data into a list
        close the file
        return the new list of student data
    end if
end procedure
```

We decided earlier that information on each student will be held in its own `list`. 26 students mean 26 `lists`. We have a collection of students so the simplest data structure to hold all 26 students is a `list` of the 26 individual student `lists` which we're now calling `studentList`. There's nothing difficult about `lists` of `lists`. As you'll see later, it's actually pretty easy to get at any one of the `lists` using an index and indeed at any of the individual fields of any particular student using a double index. For example, we can get at the third student's data using `studentData[2]`, in this case Versa Smith's information and we can get directly at her telephone number using `studentData[2][5]`.

There are a number of ways to open files in Python, but we'll use the simplest form using the `open` function which returns a *file object*. We use the file object to load data from our file line by line. We do need to check that we don't get an error when we try to open the file, so we'll use Python's exception handling to do this. If the data is loaded successfully we'll return the list of students to the section of code that called us and close the file. If the file is missing, we'll say so.

This pseudo code translates pretty directly into Python. The first thing we need to do is to import the `csv` library in order to make use of the `reader` function from the library. We could use the statement `from csv import reader` and then we could refer to `reader` without prefixing it with `csv`. Personally, we prefer not to do this. As we explained earlier, by simply using `import csv` we're obliged to prefix `reader` with `csv` in order to use the function. This has the downside of a little more typing but the upside is that we can see at a glance where the function comes from which is good from a maintenance point of view.

Inside our `loadStudentData` function, we use the Python `try` ...`except` ...`else` ... construct to check if we can open the file. If we fail for some reason, perhaps the file is missing or damaged, we'll print a message and return an empty list. Otherwise, we'll continue in the `else` clause, print a message to say that we opened the file successfully, create a new empty list called `students` and then using the `csv.reader` function, read each line in turn, appending each line to the ever growing `students` list. We finish off by closing the file and returning our new **students** list to the calling program. Note that this tiny program assumes that the text file `students.csv` is in the same directory as our program. If not, we'll get an error.

Listing 4.3: Load the student data file (loadStudentData.py)

```
import csv

def loadStudentData():
    try:
        f = open("students.csv", "r")

    except IOError as e:
        print("Failed to open data file")
        return []

    else:
        print("Students data file opened successfully")
        students = []
        for line in csv.reader(f):
          students.append(line)
        f.close()
        return students

# main program starts here
StudentList = loadStudentData()
```

When you run the program you should get a message saying the file loaded successfully. We're pretty confident that everything is working, but to be absolutely certain that we've loaded the data successfully, we really should show what has been loaded. So let's create a display function which we'll call `displayList(L)` where `L` is the list we want displayed, which in this instance will be list returned to us by `loadStudentData`. Note that the first line of our pseudo code checks that the list we've been given isn't empty before we try to read it - that's always good programming practice. The pseudo code shown in 4.4 is fairly self explanatory.

PseudoCode 4.4 Display list

```
Require: List L
procedure DISPLAY LIST
    if L isn't empty then
        for each list in L do                ▷ each list represents one student
            print list
        end for
    else
        print "List is empty"
    end if
end procedure
```

A practice that we've adopted throughout this book is that when we write a new function we'll usually include other code that's necessary to run and very importantly test the code, which makes the code look somewhat larger than it is. As you can see here, the code for displaying the list in the function `displayList` in the python file `showStudentData.py` is actually very short and is pretty much line for line the same as the pseudo code.

Listing 4.4: Show the StudentData (showStudentData.py)

```
import csv

def displayList(L):
    if L != []:
        for s in L:
            print (s)
    else:
        print("List is empty")

def loadStudentData():
# start by trying to load our data file.
    try:
        f = open("students.csv", "r")

    except IOError as e:
        print("Failed to open data file")
        return []

    else:
        print("Students data file opened successfully")
        students = []
        for line in csv.reader(f):
          students.append(line)
        f.close()
        return students

# main program starts here
studentList = loadStudentData()
displayList(studentList)
```

All being well, when you run this program you should see 26 lines of student information printed to the screen.

So, what have we achieved so far? We've used a text editor to create 26 students packed with information that Mr Leeman needs for his little database. We've written a function `loadStudentData` to load this file which returns whatever it found on the disk in the form of a `list`. We've written a function `displayList` to display what the data looks like when it's been loaded into our program. We've not tackled directly any of the functions that Mr Leeman wants written but as you'll see shortly, doing so will now be much,

much easier.

Let's start by drawing a diagram. It would be useful to get some sort of idea of exactly what functions need to be written and how they're going to be connected. This is still pretty provisional at this stage, but a simple drawing would be quite useful. We'd normally draw this by hand but given that we've got some very powerful software tools at our disposal we'll make it a little prettier.

Figure 4.2: Life Cycle with Functions

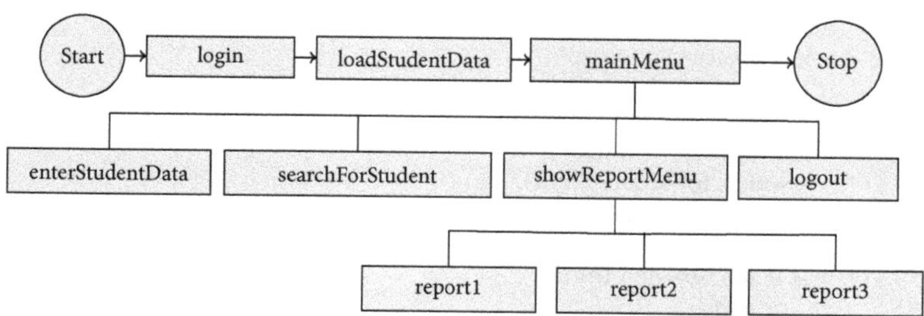

This drawing is a sort of mish mash of life cycle and functions needed. We're going to Start, login, load some data (if it exists) and then enter the main menu code. In the main menu we'll be able to enter data on a new student, search for a student based on the unique ID, show a report menu and logout, in which case unless we need to tidy up in any way, we might jump immediately to Stop. In the report menu we're going to create three different reports. That seems to cover everything that Mr Leeman wants from us.

We've written the login function and we've written a function to load any existing data. We've also written a helper function to show the contents of any list that we're holding in memory. This leaves us with eight functions to write. Let's start with the main menu.

4.4 Main menu

Mr Leeman wants a simple menu interface and another menu to select one of the three reports. A simple main menu is shown below. It makes sense to include logging out as one of the menu options and we may have to do some 'cleaning up', i.e. saving data etc., so we'll need a separate `logout()` function.

1. Enter new student information
2. Search for student
3. Create a report
4. Logout

If Mr Leeman selects option 3 to "Create a report", that should lead to a second menu with the three reports itemised. At some point we'll need to consider what three reports Mr Leeman might like to see, but let's leave that for the moment.

We can now take a more detailed look at the function `mainMenu`. The simplest way to approach this is to write it in pseudo-code which you should then be able to code pretty quickly.

PseudoCode 4.5 Main menu

```
procedure MAIN MENU
    while true do
        draw the main menu
        select option
        if option = 1 then
            enter new student information
        else if option = 2 then
            search for student by ID
        else if option = 3 then
            open the report menu
        else if option = 4 then
            return
        else if option = 0 then
            display the current state of the studentList
        else
            print "You've not selected a valid option"
        end if
    end while
end procedure
```

This captures the essence of what Mr Leeman wants to do. The neatest way to move to coding this is to write a new program that consists of a single function with 'placeholder' functions for each of the options. Placeholder functions are functions that don't actually do anything - yet. They're there to remind us that we'll have to fill them in later and they let us get a little program up and running and tested quickly. Note that we intend staying inside the main menu until option 4 is selected in which case we can simply `return` to the main code. The cleanest way to do this is to simply say `while True` which effectively means forever.

All that the placeholder functions need to do at this stage is tell us that they've been called. We'll write these functions one by one later as the code develops. At the moment we simply want to get the menu function working. We're going to call `mainMenu` and it's going to call three placeholder functions

- `enterNewStudentInformation`
- `searchForStudentByID`
- `reportMenu`

that simply print their name, indicating that they've been called. The important thing is to write code to select one of the options, leaving if we select the **Logout** option and putting up a simple message if Mr Leeman hits a key that doesn't represent one of the available options.

The more eagle-eyed amongst you will have noticed that we've added a fifth option which displays the current state of our **studentList** if we enter a 0. We're not going to tell the user this, so we won't display it in our main menu but it'll still be there, hidden in the background and it'll be triggered if we hit 0. Why are we doing this? Quite simply, it's really useful to be able to check on the state of our data structures whenever we want so having a hidden 'back door' into the software to show us what is going on can only be a good thing.

Listing 4.5: Main menu (mainMenu.py)

```
def displayList(L):
    if L != []:
        for s in L:
            print (s)
    else:
        print("List is empty")

def enterNewStudentInformation(L):
    print ('-- enterNewStudentInformation --')

def searchForStudentByID(L):
    print ('-- searchForStudentByID --')

def reportMenu(L):
    print ('-- reportMenu --')

def mainMenu(L):
    while True:
        print ('1. Enter new student information')
        print ('2. Search by ID')
        print ('3. Report Menu')
        print ('4. Logout')

        option = input('Select an option : ')
        if option == '1':
            enterNewStudentInformation(L)
        elif option == '2':
            searchForStudentByID(L)
        elif option == '3':
            reportMenu(L)
        elif option == '4':
            return
        elif option == '0':
```

```
            displayList(L)
        else:
            print ('Not a valid choice - try again')

# main program starts here
StudentList = []
mainMenu(StudentList)
```

One thing to pay attention to is that just before we call our main menu we're creating an empty `studentList`. In the final program the first thing we'll do is to load the student data (if any) that we've got stored on the hard disk. Because the functions that are called by the main menu will be operating on this data we need to pass `studentList` to `mainMenu` so that it can pass the list on in turn to the other functions. Passing and returning data from functions is an essential part of programming, otherwise we'd have to use global variables and global variables are in the main to be avoided, as we explain in the programming style section on page 3.4.

Notice also that we've *not* included the code for logging in that we wrote previously. The essence of our approach is to take small steps, work out what we want to do, write some pseudo-code, write some code to test some particular function, including placeholder functions. If we had included the login code that we wrote earlier, every time we ran the program we'd have to log in before being able to do anything else. This is perhaps a small point, but it'll slow development quite a bit. When we've written all of the functions needed for the project, we'll gather everything together in a single program for final system testing.

Run this little program and test it by checking that each of the available options work exactly as described. The three placeholder functions should tell us that they've been called and if we select option 4 the program should exit gracefully. If you select the secret option 0 you'll get a message telling you correctly that the list is currently empty.

4.4.1 Student information - what type of data

According to the scenario, Mr Leeman wants student data that consists of a *unique ID*, *surname*, *forename*, *date of birth*, *home address*, *home phone number*, *gender*, *tutor group* and unique *school email address* for each student. If we were creating a commercial program for Mr Leeman we'd have to worry about validating and ideally verifying any data that he enters but for our purposes, excepting the email address as described below, we're simply going to accept anything that we're offered.

The scenario says that every student is given a unique ID and a unique email address when they enter the school so we're going to assume that uniqueness will have already been assured. It probably makes sense to assume that given that the school has gone to the trouble of assigning a unique ID it'll re-use the ID in the email address which will also guarantee its uniqueness. We can assume that IDs are integers, perhaps something like 158 or 212289 so we might expect to find corresponding email addresses of

`158@treeroad.sch.uk` and `212289@treeroad.sch.uk`.

This suggests that once Mr Leeman has entered a student's unique ID, we can simply concatenate the ID with `@treeroad.sch.uk` to create a unique email address. With that in mind, we can now move on and write the code to allow Mr Leeman to enter a new student's information.

4.4.2 Entering Student Details

In this function which we've previously called `enterNewStudentInformation`, we'll be passed the current `studentList`. We'll create a new empty list, let's call it `s`. We'll ask Mr Leeman field by field, uniqueID first, then surname and so on for details of the student which we'll append one by one to `s`. When Mr Leeman has finished entering everything, we'll append `s` to the list we were given and return it to the main menu code. The pseudo code is quite straightforward.

PseudoCode 4.6 Enter new student information

Require: list L

procedure ENTER NEW STUDENT INFORMATION
    Create a new empty list called s
    Ask for and append the unique ID to s
    Ask for and append the surname to s
    Ask for and append the forename to s
    Ask for and append the date of birth to s
    Ask for and append the home address to s
    Ask for and append the home address to s
    Ask for and append the phone number to s
    Ask for and append the gender to s
    Ask for and append the tutor group to s
    Construct and append the unique email address to s
    Append s to the list L that we were given
    return L
end procedure

The code for this function follows the pseudo code very closely. Note that we've been passed the current list of students. This list will be empty if there's currently no data but it's perfectly fine to **append** to an empty list.

Listing 4.6: Enter new Student Information (enterNewStudentInformation.py)

```
def displayList(L):
    if L != []:
        for s in L:
            print (s)
    else:
```

```
        print("List is empty")

def enterNewStudentInformation(L):
    s = []
    uniqueID = input("Unique ID: ")
    s.append(uniqueID)
    surname = input("Surname: ")
    s.append(surname)
    forename = input("Forename: ")
    s.append(forename)
    dob = input("Date of Birth [dd-mm-yyyy]: ")
    s.append(dob)
    address = input("Home address: ")
    s.append(address)
    phone = input("Phone number: ")
    s.append(phone)
    gender = input("Gender [M/F]: ")
    s.append(gender)
    group = input("Tutor group : ")
    s.append(group)
    s.append(str(uniqueID) + "@treeroad.sch.uk")

    L.append(s)

    return L

def searchForStudentByID(L):
    print ('-- searchForStudentByID --')

def reportMenu(L):
    print ('-- reportMenu --')

def mainMenu(L):
    while True:
        print ('1. Enter new student information')
        print ('2. Search by ID')
        print ('3. Report Menu')
        print ('4. Logout')

        option = input('Select an option : ')
        if option == '1':
            enterNewStudentInformation(L)
        elif option == '2':
            searchForStudentByID(L)
        elif option == '3':
            reportMenu(L)
        elif option == '4':
            return
        elif option == '0':
```

```
            displayList(L)
        else:
            print ('Not a valid choice - try again')

# main program starts here
StudentList = []
mainMenu(StudentList)
```

We ran this on our computer, selecting first our secret option 0 to show that **studentList** was empty when we started. We then selected option 1 and entered some information on a new student. We selected 0 again to check that the new data had made its way into **studentList** and finally we logged out by selecting option 4.

Program Output

```
1. Enter new student information
2. Search by ID
3. Report Menu
4. Logout
Select an option : 0
List is empty
1. Enter new student information
2. Search by ID
3. Report Menu
4. Logout
Select an option : 1
Unique ID: 234234
Surname: Arbuthnott
Forename: Charles
Date of Birth [dd-mm-yyyy]: 12-12-2001
Home address: 57 The crescent, London, NW10 3BY
Phone number: 0121 7895674
Gender [M/F]: M
Tutor group : 5LM
1. Enter new student information
2. Search by ID
3. Report Menu
4. Logout
Select an option : 0
[234234, 'Arbuthnott', 'Charles', '12-12-2001', '57 The crescent, London,
NW10 3BY', '0121 7895674', 'M', '5LM', '234234@treeroad.sch.uk']
1. Enter new student information
2. Search by ID
3. Report Menu
4. Logout
Select an option : 4
```

4.4.3 Retrieving Student Details

To retrieve a student's details Mr Leeman has to enter their unique ID given to them when they entered the school. This isn't a particularly sensible way of getting student data since it means that poor Mr Leeman has to remember the unique IDs of all of his students. Using their surnames instead is far more sensible. That said, this does however give us a suggestion for one of the reports at least - a list of students in alphabetical order together with their unique IDs. He'd need such a list to retrieve their data. Let's suppose that either he has such a list or he has a brilliant memory and we can then get on with the scenario.

What do we have to do?

First off, we need to ask Mr Leeman for the unique ID which we then try to match against the list of IDs in our little database. If we find a match, we'll display the data in a suitable fashion, if not, we'll display a message telling him that there was no such ID. In pseudo code:

PseudoCode 4.7 Search for Student by ID

```
Require: List L
procedure SEARCH FOR STUDENT BY ID
    if the list we've been given is not empty then
        Ask for a unique ID
        for each student in the list do
            if the ID matches a student ID then
                Display the student's details
                return
            end if
        end for
        Print "Sorry, no match found"
    else
        "Print "List is empty"
    end if
end procedure
```

Hopefully you will recall that the unique ID is held in the first field of every student record. We'll need this in the code that follows.

Listing 4.7: Search for student by ID (searchForStudentByID.py)

```
import csv

def loadStudentData():
    try:
        f = open("students.csv", "r")

```

```
    except IOError as e:
        print("Failed to open data file")
        return []

    else:
        print("Students data file opened successfully")
        students = []
        for line in csv.reader(f):
          students.append(line)
        f.close()
        return students

def displayList(L):
    if L != []:
        for s in L:
            print (s)
    else:
        print("List is empty")

def enterNewStudentInformation(L):
    print ('-- enterNewStudentInformation --')

def searchForStudentByID(L):
    if L != []:
        uniqueID = int(input("Please enter a unique ID: "))
        for s in L:
            if int(s[0]) == uniqueID:
                print ("Found " + str(s))
                return

        # if we've tried every student in StudentList
        print("Sorry, couldn't find a match")
    else:
        print("No student data found")

def reportMenu(L):
    print ('-- reportMenu --')

def mainMenu(L):
    while True:
        print ('1. Enter new student information')
        print ('2. Search by ID')
        print ('3. Report Menu')
        print ('4. Logout')

        option = input('Select an option : ')
        if option == '1':
            enterNewStudentInformation(L)
        elif option == '2':
```

```
            searchForStudentByID(L)
        elif option == '3':
            reportMenu(L)
        elif option == '4':
            return
        elif option == '0':
            displayList(L)
        else:
            print ('Not a valid choice - try again')

# main program starts here
StudentList = loadStudentData()
mainMenu(StudentList)
```

In order to test this function we need to show that it works correctly if no ID matches and also if an ID does match. To show that an ID doesn't match all we need do is select option 2 and pick an arbitrary integer. To show that it does match we could either select option 1, enter some data and then select option 2 with the unique ID that we've just entered for the new student or alternatively, we could load the external student data file and pick an ID that exists amongst the 24 students in the data file. It's quicker and easier to use the second option.

The following few lines show the results of testing with IDs of 111232 and 2231. In the first case there's no match, in the second this corresponds to `Trevor Owen`.

Program Output

```
Students data file opened successfully
1. Enter new student information
2. Search by ID
3. Report Menu
4. Logout
Select an option : 2
Please enter a unique ID: 111232
Sorry, couldn't find a match
1. Enter new student information
2. Search by ID
3. Report Menu
4. Logout
Select an option : 2
Please enter a unique ID: 2231
Found ['2231', 'Owen', 'Trevor', '18-05-2003', '5 Marsh Lane, Marston,
Oxford, OX3 2TY', '0186520453', 'M', '5LM', '2231@treeroad.sch.uk']
1. Enter new student information
2. Search by ID
3. Report Menu
4. Logout
Select an option : 4
```

Have we answered *'retrieve and display the details of any student when Mr Leeman enters the student's unique ID number'* correctly? We've certainly displayed the information, not necessarily as prettily as one might like, but it's perfectly serviceable so let's get on with the next section - reports.

4.4.4 Creating Reports

Mr Leeman wants to select reports. We know how to make a menu and this time he wants to select three reports. What reports shall we give him? The scenario simply asks for three different reports so let's think.

As we pointed out earlier, the scenario asks that Mr Leeman can search for a student's details based on their unique ID. If you'd asked someone to do this in real life, they're unlikely to be impressed since it's pretty tricky to try to remember 25+ unique IDs. Just as we can remember to type in Google rather than Google's IP address, currently 216.58.206.78 according to my DNS lookup, it's far easier to remember student's names rather than their unique ID. In which case, a report that simply displays surname and unique ID would be pretty useful for Mr Leeman. Ideally the list of surnames should be in alphabetical order.

So, report number one will display `surname, unique ID` in alphabetical order. Let's write some pseudo code to do that now.

PseudoCode 4.8 Report 1 - surname and unique ID

```
Require: List L                                        ▷ i.e. current student list
procedure REPORT 1
    Create an empty list, call it report
    if L isn't empty then
        for each student in L do
            Create an empty list; call it r
            Append each student's name to r
            Append each student's ID to r
            Append r to report
        end for
        Sort report alphabetically according to surname
    end if
    return report
end procedure
```

This looks pretty straightforward. We'll pass the current `StudentList`to our function and we'll immediately create an empty list called `report` that we'll return to the main menu. We'll check that `L` isn't empty. If it is we'll simply return an empty list to the calling function. If not, as we run through the code, `report` will become a sorted list of elements, each of which will be a `list` holding the surname and unique ID of each student (in that order). To make this happen, for each student in the list we'll create a new empty `list` called `r` to which we'll append first the surname and then the unique ID. We'll append every `r` (we'll make as many `r` lists as there are students) to `report`. Once we've run through the complete list of students we'll sort `report` into alphabetical order on surname and return the new sorted list to the main menu. In code that you can run, this looks like:

Listing 4.8: Report 1 surname and unique ID (report1.py)

```
import csv

def displayList(L):
    if L != []:
        for s in L:
            print (s)
    else:
        print("List is empty")

def loadStudentData():
# start by trying to load our data file.
    try:
        f = open("students.csv", "r")

    except IOError as e:
        print("Failed to open data file")
        return []

    else:
        print("Students data file opened successfully")
        students = []
        for line in csv.reader(f):
            students.append(line)
        f.close()
        return students

def report1(L):
    report = []
    if L != []:
        for s in L:
            r = []
            r.append(s[1])
            r.append(s[0])
            report.append(r)

        report = sorted(report, key = lambda student: student[0])

    return report

# main program starts here
StudentList = loadStudentData()
```

```
42  r = report1(StudentList)
43  displayList(r)
```

As you can see, it follows the pseudo code pretty exactly and is actually pretty short. Let's go through the code line by line.

We start by loading our example data file. This data is loaded into `StudentList`. which is passed into `report1` and a new empty list called `report` is created. If `StudentList` isn't empty - it won't be if we loaded the example data successfully, we create a temporary `list r` and loop through all students in `StudentList`, selecting and appending the surname and unique ID at indices 1 and 0 respectively to `r`. When we've been through all of the students in `StudentList` we'll drop out of the `for` loop with `report` holding a list of tuples of every student's information in the form `['surname', 'unique ID']`. We then execute line 39 which sorts `report` using the library function `sorted` which takes two parameters, (1) the name of the `list` we want to sort and (2) which field we want to sort the report on. We appended surname and unique ID to `r` specifically in that order which means that the field at position 0 in every tuple holds the surname, whilst the unique ID is at position 1. It looks complicated but hopefully not too tricky to get your head around. When called like this `sorted` returns us a sorted list which it puts back into `report`

Finally we return `report` to the main body of our code.

Note that we've used our utility function `loadStudentData(L)` to load our example student data file - see how useful it is to have example data available? We've also made use of `displayList(L)` which simply displays any list of lists that it's given. In this case we can give it the report data that our function `report1` has returned to us. Again, this little function is proving to be very useful.

The output (truncated a little) from this little program is as follows.

Program Output

```
Students data file opened successfully
['Acha', '91']
['Arbuthnott', '1123']
['Bell', '11267']
['Bora', '967']
['Gras', '443']
['Gras', '5542']
...
['Spoor', '321']
['Tomas', '17893']
['Toms', '1321']
['Toole', '3468']
['Williams', '14356']
```

Let's move on. What shall we do for report number two? We have a number of options, but probably the next most useful for Mr Leeman would be to have a separate list of all of the boys and all of the girls and again alphabetical order would be nice so let's do that.

To produce a list of all of the boys we're going to look at all of the students, segregating them into two lists, one where gender is "M" which indicates a boy and one where gender is "F" which indicates a girl. It's going to be very similar to the pseudo code that we wrote for the first report except that we're going to return two lists, one for boys and one for girls. We should probably include each student's first name and surname and we might as well add their unique ID for good measure. We'll store the information in the order *surname, first name, uniqueID*. As with report 1 we'll sort on surname which again will be at index 0. Note that since the first thing that we do is to create two empty lists, one called `boys`, the other called `girls`, if we've been passed an empty list, we'll return two empty lists.

PseudoCode 4.9 Report 2 - boys and girls

```
Require: List L                                        ▷ i.e. current student list
procedure REPORT 2
    Create two empty lists, call them boys and girls
    if L isn't empty then
        for each student in L do
            Create an empty list; call it r
            Append the student's surname to r
            Append the student's forename to r
            Append the student's unique ID to r
            if the student's gender is "m" or "M" then
                Append r to boys
            else if the student's gender is "f" or "F" then
                Append r to girls
            else
                Print "Missing gender for student with unique ID" uniqueID
            end if
        end for
        Sort boys alphabetically according to surname
        Sort girls alphabetically according to surname
    end if
    return boys and girls
end procedure
```

The code is very similar to the pseudo code. As we mentioned earlier, we deliberately left out some data for some students and in one case we left out the gender information. The lines of code that check gender will add the student to the `boys` list if gender is either 'm' or 'M' and similarly add the student to the `girls` list if gender is either 'f' or 'F'. If these tests fail the code should print out a message telling us which student did not have their gender listed.

Listing 4.9: Report 2 - boys and girls (report2.py)

```
import csv

def displayList(L):
    if L != []:
        for s in L:
            print (s)
    else:
        print("List is empty")

def loadStudentData():
# start by trying to load our data file.
    try:
        f = open("students.csv", "r")

    except IOError as e:
        print("Failed to open data file")
        return []

    else:
        print("Students data file opened successfully")
        students = []
        for line in csv.reader(f):
            students.append(line)
        f.close()
        return students

def report2(L):
    boys = []
    girls = []

    if L != []:
        for s in L:
            r = []
            r.append(s[1])
            r.append(s[2])
            r.append(s[0])

            if s[6] in ['m','M']:
                boys.append(r)
            elif s[6] in ['f','F']:
                girls.append(r)
            else:
                print ("Missing gender for student with unique ID " + s[0])

        boys = sorted(boys, key = lambda student: student[0])
        girls = sorted(girls, key = lambda student: student[0])

```

```
    return boys, girls

# main program starts here
StudentList = loadStudentData()
boys, girls = report2(StudentList)
print("Boys")
displayList(boys)
print("Girls")
displayList(girls)
```

When you run this with our data you should get the following with each student information on its own line.

Program Output

```
Students data file opened successfully
Missing gender for student with unique ID 2211
Missing gender for student with unique ID 876876
Boys
['Acha', 'Nero', '91']
['Arbuthnott', 'Charlie', '1123']
['Bora', 'Zarek', '967']
['Gras', 'Ossie', '443']
['Long', 'Albert', '22113']
['Owen', 'Trevor', '2231']
['Parker', 'Peter', '23876']
['Peters', 'Will', '67']
['Tomas', 'Tim', '17893']
['Toole', 'Peter', '3468']
['Williams', 'Tom', '14356']
Girls
['Bell', 'Mischa', '11267']
['Gras', 'Hannah', '5542']
['Herbert', 'Liz', '2238']
['Hignam', 'Megan', '4452']
['Mosel', 'Eva', '17112']
['Patel', 'Aya', '324']
['Patel', 'Simla', '66733']
['Pears', 'Anwen', '4563']
['Preston', 'Elinor', '2900']
['Priest', 'May', '22978']
['Smith', 'Versa', '21789']
['Smith', 'Mary', '78932']
['Spoor', 'Evie', '321']
['Toms', 'Lisa', '1321']
```

Hopefully if you've understood the code for `report1` in listing 4.8 you'll have understood listing 4.9. It looks more complicated with the rest of the code around it but you should be familiar with that code too. In which case, let's write the last report.

If you look carefully at the student data that we've created there are mistakes and some fields are empty. This is very common in real life and assuming that Mr Leeman is like most people, he's unlikely to have created a perfect list of student information. He'll have made mistakes and quite possibly the information wasn't available to him when he created it. In either case it would be very useful if he could get a list of missing data. Each student has nine fields of data associated with them. A useful report will tell Mr Leeman what fields are empty for each of the students.

So, let's produce a print out of each student and if any fields are empty, we'll give the index of those fields. The sort of thing that we have in mind is a report which would include something like the following example.

```
['Peter', 'Parker']
['Tim', 'Tomas', '5']
['Hanna', 'Gras', '4', '5']
```

In this example, Peter Parker's data is complete - nothing is missing. Tim Tomas on the other hand is missing the field with index 5, i.e. his telephone number and Hanna Gras is missing data at indices 4 and 5, i.e. address and telephone number.

The pseudo code to produce this report looks like this.

PseudoCode 4.10 Report 3 - missing data

```
Require: List L                                          ▷ i.e. current student list
procedure REPORT 3
    Create an empty list, call it report
    if L isn't empty then
        for each student in L do
            Create an empty list; call it r
            Append each student's forename to r
            Append each student's surname to r
            for each field in L do
                if any field is empty then
                    Append it's index to r
                end if
            end for
            Append r to report
        end for
    end if
    return report
end procedure
```

The code for this report function follows the pseudo code pretty much line for line and is very similar to the previous two reports. The program to test this is the following.

Listing 4.10: Report3 missing data (report3.py)

```
import csv

def displayList(L):
    if L != []:
        for s in L:
            print (s)
    else:
        print("List is empty")

def loadStudentData():
# start by trying to load our data file.
    try:
        f = open("students.csv", "r")

    except IOError as e:
        print("Failed to open data file")
        return []

    else:
        print("Students data file opened successfully")
        students = []
        for line in csv.reader(f):
            students.append(line)
        f.close()
        return students

def report3(L):
    report = []

    if L != None:
        for s in L:
            r = []
            r.append(s[2])
            r.append(s[1])

            for i in range(9):
                if (s[i] == ""):
                    r.append(str(i))

            report.append(r)

    return report

# main program starts here
StudentList = loadStudentData()
report = report3(StudentList)
displayList(report)
```

Hopefully you can now see just how useful it has been to have written the two small functions `displayList` and `loadStudentData` early on in the development process. It is often difficult to see what is going on in software and to have simple utility functions that can load example data for you to play with and print out information on your data structures is time that repays itself many times over during the course of development.

It's also quite interesting to see how small the actual report function is. In fact, all three report functions are pretty small.

If you're using our data you should get the following display.

Program Output

```
Students data file opened successfully
['Peter', 'Parker']
['Tim', 'Tomas', '5']
['Versa', 'Smith']
['Nero', 'Acha']
['Tom', 'Williams']
['Aya', 'Patel']
['Eva', 'Mosel']
['Anwen', 'Pears']
['Elinor', 'Preston', '5']
['Mischa', 'Bell', '5']
['Albert', 'Long']
['Evie', 'Spoor']
['Mary', 'Smith']
['Simla', 'Patel', '3']
['Trevor', 'Owen']
['Ossie', 'Gras']
['May', 'Priest']
['Lisa', 'Toms', '4', '5']
['Liz', 'Herbert', '5']
['Hannah', 'Gras', '4', '5']
['Megan', 'Hignam']
['Peter', 'Toole']
['Zarek', 'Bora']
['Will', 'Peters', '4']
['Charlie', 'Arbuthnott']
['Mary', 'Peters', '6']
['Arnold', 'Peters', '6']
```

That's the third report competed. Now we need to tie everything together in one program and test it thoroughly. We've not written the menu for the three reports so let's do that now. We'll arrive at the report menu via one of the options in the main menu. We'll need three options for each of the reports and a fourth option to return to the main menu. Our menu will be passed a copy of the current `studentList` to play with but will pass back nothing. The pseudo code for this function, let's call it reportMenu should be something like the following.

PseudoCode 4.11 Report menu

```
procedure REPORT MENU
    while true do
        Draw the report menu
        Select option
        if option = 1 then
            Create Report 1
        else if option = 2 then
            Create Report 2
        else if option = 3 then
            Create Report 3
        else if option = 4 then
            return
        else
            print "You've not selected a valid option"
        end if
    end while
end procedure
```

The code for this menu is almost the same as the code for the main menu at listing 4.5 on page 39.

Listing 4.11: Report Menu (reportMenu.py)

```
def report1(L):
    print ('-- report 1 --')

def report2(L):
    print ('-- report 2 --')

def report3(L):
    print ('-- report 3 --')

def reportMenu(L):
  while True:
    print ('1. Create report to match unique ID to surname')
    print ('2. Create report to identify girls and boys')
    print ('3. Create report to identify missing information')
    print ('4. Return to main menu')

    option = input('Select an option : ')
    if option == '1':
      report1(L)
    elif option == '2':
      report2(L)
    elif option == '3':
      report3(L)
```

```
    elif option == '4':
      return
    else:
      print ('Not a valid choice - try again')

# main program starts here
reportMenu([])
```

This works perfectly well as a simple stand alone program. All we need to do now is to put all of the functions together in one file and make sure that all of the calls are correct.

To recap, figure 4.3 below shows the functions that we've written and their connectivity. For example, our `mainMenu` function calls `enterNewStudentInformation`, `searchForStudentByID`, `reportMenu` and `logout`. `reportMenu` in turn will call `report1`, `report2` and `report3`. The top line shows the life cycle of the project. We `Start`, `login`, `loadStudentData` and draw our `mainMenu` from which we can select options 1 through 4. If option 4 is selected we call `logout` and we `Stop`.

Figure 4.3: Life Cycle with Functions

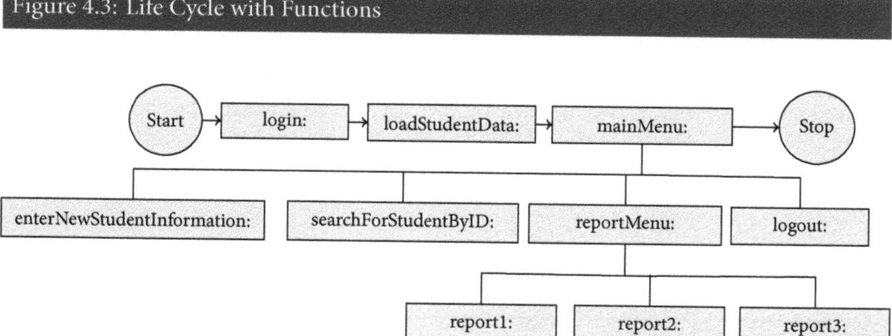

Figure 4.3 does not show our little utility function `displayList`. By writing the two utility (i.e. useful) functions `loadStudentData` and `displayList` early on in the project, every time we wrote a new function we were able to write a small program to load an example data file and test what was happening in our function by displaying `StudentList`. Doing this made development much clearer, much faster and much easier.

Breaking a problem down into little pieces, each of which can be independently written and tested is an incredibly important skill to learn as a programmer. Pretty much all problems are way too big to solve by simply sitting in front of your computer and writing code. Except with tiny programs, that approach is a recipe for disaster. It's much more important before starting on a new project to sit and quietly work out with pen and paper what it is that you need doing. Pretty diagrams look nice, but when professional programmers are breaking problems apart they doodle, they write bits of pseudo code, they might draw some flow charts or they might simply make odd scratches on the paper. What they're doing is thinking and thinking is done best with a pencil in your hand and paper in front of you.

With that out of the way there's still a very important function to write before we tie everything together: logging out. Usually the first thing that we should do once Mr Leeman has logged in is to try to load an already existing data file. If it doesn't exist, presumably because it's the first time that Mr Leeman has run the program, that shouldn't present us with any difficulties and indeed one would expect that the first thing that Mr Leeman would then do is to enter some student data which will then be saved in a newly created `StudentList`. But what should we do when he's finished his editing and selects the `logout` option. There's no option to save any data and presumably he'd really like to know that all of his hard work has not gone in vain. Ideally, when he next logs in all of the data that he entered ever so painfully earlier should still be available to him. This means that we need to write a good `logout` function that does the really important job of saving our data, i.e. `StudentList`.

In order to minimize any potential loss of data it's good practice to keep a backup file in addition to the current data. That suggests that when we logout we should rename any current `students.csv` file as a backup file, say as `students.backup`, making sure to delete any backup file first if it exists. If the backup file has been created safely, we can then save whatever we're holding in memory to a new `students.csv` file. In this way we've always got two copies of relevant data just in case anything goes wrong. Note that if our student list is currently empty, i.e. we have no data in memory, we can exit immediately without bothering with any files.

If we follow the logic above, the pseudo code to do this would be as follows.

PseudoCode 4.12 Logout

```
Require: List L                                   ▷ i.e. current student list
procedure LOGOUT
    if L isn't empty then
        if students.csv exists then
            if students.backup exists then
                Delete students.backup
            end if
            Rename students.csv to students.backup
        end if
        Create a new students.csv
        Write all the data in L to students.csv
        Close the file
    end if
end procedure
```

We're going to make use of some of the os library functions. The ones of particular interest to us are `os.path.isfile(filename)` which returns `True` if filename exists and `False` otherwise and `os.remove(filename)` which does exactly as it's name suggests. The third function, `os.rename(fileA, fileB)` renames `fileA` to `fileB`.

Since we're going to save our file in the same CSV format that we loaded the file, we'll use the `csv` library function `csv.writer` and the `writerows` function. Translating the pseudo code into runnable code is also fairly straightforward. We've added some messages that will get printed to the screen to let Mr Leeman know what we've done.

Listing 4.12: Logout (logout.py)

```
import os
import csv

def loadStudentData():
# start by trying to load our data file.
    try:
        f = open("students.csv", "r")

    except IOError as e:
        print("Failed to open data file")
        return []

    else:
        print("Students data file opened successfully")
        students = []
        for line in csv.reader(f):
          students.append(line)
        f.close()
        return students

def logout(L):
    print ("Logging out ...")
    if L != []:
        if os.path.isfile("students.csv"):
            if os.path.isfile("students.backup"):
                os.remove("students.backup")
                print ("students backup file has been deleted")

            os.rename("students.csv", "students.backup")
            print ("Students data file has been renamed to 'students.backup'")

        f = open("students.csv", "w")
        writer = csv.writer(f)
        writer.writerows(L)
        f.close()

        print ("Student data has been saved successfully in 'students.csv'")
```

```python

    else:
        print ("No data to save")

# main program starts here
StudentList = loadStudentData()
logout(StudentList)
```

That's it for the individual functions. It's now a relatively straightforward matter to tie all of these together into a working program. There's lots that we can do to improve it but in the meantime, here's the code for a complete working version of the project.

Listing 4.13: Complete code (sample1.py)

```python
import os
import csv

MR_LEEMANS_USERNAME = 'pleeman'
MR_LEEMANS_PASSWORD = 'abcd1234'

def loginWasSuccessful():
    username = input("Hello, please enter your username: ")
    if username == MR_LEEMANS_USERNAME:
        counter = 0
        while counter < 3:
            password = input("Hello Mr. Leeman, please enter your password: ")
            if password == MR_LEEMANS_PASSWORD:
                return True
            else:
                counter = counter + 1

    return False

def displayList(L):
    if L != []:
        for s in L:
            print (s)
    else:
        print("List is empty")

def loadStudentData():
# start by trying to load our data file.
    try:
        f = open("students.csv", "r")

    except IOError as e:
        print("Failed to open data file")
        return []

```

```
    else:
        print("Students data file opened successfully")
        students = []
        for line in csv.reader(f):
          students.append(line)
        f.close()
        return students

def logout(L):
    print ("Logging out ...")
    if L != []:
        if os.path.isfile("students.csv"):
            if os.path.isfile("students.backup"):
                os.remove("students.backup")
                print ("students backup file has been removed")

            os.rename("students.csv", "students.backup")
            print ("Students data file has been renamed to 'students.backup'")

        f = open("students.csv", "w")
        writer = csv.writer(f)
        writer.writerows(L)
        f.close()

        print ("Student data has been saved in file 'students.csv'")

    else:
        print ("No data to save")

def report1(L):
    report = []
    if L != []:
        for s in L:
            r = []
            r.append(s[1])
            r.append(s[0])
            report.append(r)

        report = sorted(report, key = lambda student: student[0])

    return report

def report2(L):
    boys = []
    girls = []

    if L != []:
        for s in L:
            r = []
```

```
            r.append(s[1])
            r.append(s[2])
            r.append(s[0])

            if s[6] in ['m','M']:
                boys.append(r)
            elif s[6] in ['f','F']:
                girls.append(r)
            else:
                print ("Missing gender for student with unique ID " + s[0])

        boys = sorted(boys, key = lambda student: student[0])
        girls = sorted(girls, key = lambda student: student[0])

    return boys, girls

def report3(L):
    report = []

    if L != None:
        for s in L:
            r = []
            r.append(s[2])
            r.append(s[1])

            for i in range(9):
                if (s[i] == ""):
                    r.append(str(i))

            report.append(r)

    return report

def reportMenu(L):
  while True:
    print ('1. Create report to match surname to unique ID')
    print ('2. Create report to identify girls and boys')
    print ('3. Create report to identify missing information')
    print ('4. Return to main menu')

    option = input('Select an option : ')
    if option == '1':
      report = report1(L)
      displayList(report)
    elif option == '2':
      boys, girls = report2(L)
      print('Boys')
      displayList(boys)
      print('Girls')
```

```
      displayList(girls)
    elif option == '3':
      report = report3(L)
      print('Missing data')
      displayList(report)
    elif option == '4':
      return
    else:
      print ('Not a valid choice - try again')

def searchForStudentByID(L):
    if L != []:
        uniqueID = int(input("Please enter a unique ID: "))
        for s in L:
            if int(s[0]) == uniqueID:
                print ("Found " + str(s))
                return

        # if we've tried every student in StudentList
        print("Sorry, couldn't find a match")
    else:
        print("No student data found")

def enterNewStudentInformation(L):
    s = []
    uniqueID = input("Unique ID: ")
    s.append(uniqueID)
    surname = input("Surname: ")
    s.append(surname)
    forename = input("Forename: ")
    s.append(forename)
    dob = input("Date of Birth [dd-mm-yyyy]: ")
    s.append(dob)
    address = input("Home address: ")
    s.append(address)
    phone = input("Phone number: ")
    s.append(phone)
    gender = input("Gender [M/F]: ")
    s.append(gender)
    group = input("Tutor group : ")
    s.append(group)
    s.append(str(uniqueID) + "@treeroad.sch.uk")

    L.append(s)
    return L

def mainMenu(L):
    while True:
        print ('1. Enter new student information')
```

```
        print ('2. Search by ID')
        print ('3. Report Menu')
        print ('4. Logout')

        option = input('Select an option : ')
        if option == '1':
            L = enterNewStudentInformation(L)
        elif option == '2':
            searchForStudentByID(L)
        elif option == '3':
            reportMenu(L)
        elif option == '4':
            return L
        elif option == '0':
            displayList(L)
        else:
            print ('Not a valid choice - try again')

# main program starts here
if loginWasSuccessful():
    StudentList = loadStudentData()
    StudentList = mainMenu(StudentList)
    logout(StudentList)
else:
    print('Apologies, but login has failed - goodbye')
```

You should now spend time checking that everything works exactly as it should. During the design phase of the project you should have had some idea of exactly what you'd want to test to ensure that everything worked properly; this should have taken the form of a test plan written out on at least one side of A4 paper. You should implement that test plan now. Since your teacher may not actually run your program he or she will want evidence that it does work. Your test plan will provide that evidence.

In addition to showing your teacher your completed test plan you should explain how you might improve it if you had the time to do so. In this particular project there's lots that we could do, for example, we could

- display information in a much more user friendly way.
- store Mr Leeman's name and password in an external file, ideally encrypted
- clear the screen each time we reprint the main and report menus
- when entering new student data
    - ensure that the unique ID is indeed unique
    - ensure that telephone numbers must have 11 digits
    - accept lower case characters 'm' and 'f' for gender
    - check that the date of birth is sensible
    - warn if items are missing
- incorporate error checking and recovery especially with reference to any external files

5

Sample Task 2

Scenario

When we use online film streaming services, such as Netflix, Blinkbox and Amazon Prime Instant Video, intelligent profiling is taking place behind the scenes.

The profiling system collects and stores all the data about the customer and their viewing choices.

The data stored is used to suggest film recommendations to the viewer.

For example, if you watch a comedy film the next recommendation you receive may include other films from that genre.

When customers sign up they create an account and must enter their details, such as:

- name
- address
- date of birth
- gender
- interests

Analyse the requirements for this system and design, develop, test and evaluate a program that:

1. enables a customer to set up an account that requires a username and a secure password* to access it.
2. stores the account information and last ten films that the customer has viewed.
3. recommends five films based on the 'genre' of previous viewings**.
4. allows a customer to choose additional viewing preferences other than 'genre'.
5. enables a customer to 'like' a film.
6. uses all of the data gathered to make recommendations for future viewing.

Note for candidates

** A secure password must contain at least one number and a capital letter.

*** The system only needs to be tested using three genres.

This looks a little like the first sample, but it's actually quite a bit trickier. As the blurb says, intelligent profiling is taking place, but real life profiling by Netflix et al uses some of the latest research in machine learning algorithms to do so. Somewhat beyond the scope of a GCSE project I'm afraid. That said, we should be able to do something interesting with a little thought and some good coding.

Where to start?

Let's go with some random thoughts for the moment.

The first item on the requirement list asks us to set up an account with some customer information to include their *name, address, date of birth, gender* and *interests*. That looks very similar to the first sample where we were asked to enter similar information on students. That proved to be pretty straightforward. We're also required to ask the customer for a username and a secure password. The task clearly wants us to validate the password to make sure that it's secure and has specified that it must include at least one number and a capital letter. Since we're simply thinking pretty freely at the moment, this immediately suggests that at some point we'll need to write a function which perhaps we'll call `passwordIsSecure()` that will return `True` or `False` accordingly. So, item 1 on the list looks OK.

Moving on, we'll need to store the account information that we've collected which means that we need to start thinking of what sort of data structure we're going to use. We'll also need to store the last ten films that the customer has viewed. Where do we get these from? The task gives us no idea unfortunately - presumably we'll have to allow the customer to enter them themselves. In item 3 we'll need to recommend five films based on the 'genre of previous viewings'. That suggests that whatever data structure we use, it'll have to include genre as well as the name of the film. Item 4 asks us to allow a customer to choose additional viewing preferences other than 'genre'. What might these be? Actors and actress names perhaps? Director's name? This suggests that whatever data structure we're going to use to keep track of the films also has to store some other information as well as genre. This is getting a little complicated.

We also need to write some code that will enable a customer to 'like' a film. That suggests adding yet another feature to information that we're keeping about our film, i.e. whether the customer liked it or not. This also means that we'll need to provide some sort of interface to allow the customer to perform the 'like' operation.

Finally, we have to use all of the data to make recommendations for future viewing (sigh). Oh, final note, we need to have at least three genres for testing purposes.

This is where we break for the moment, grab a cup of coffee, put our feet up and start doodling with some ideas.

5.1 What data structure?

As with sample one, but in this case even more so, this scenario is all about data and absolutely everything that we write will revolve around the data structure that we choose to hold our data. It's imperative that we think this one through really, really carefully before we try to write any code. So let's quickly recap.

According to the scenario, a customer account must hold the customer's *name*, *address*, *date of birth*, *gender* and *interests*. We're also going to have to keep track of their *username* and *password*. That suggests a total of 7 items. Each of the items represents a single item with the exception of interests where we really should assume that *interests* means a `list` of interests such as `["films","music","tv", "friends"] and so on`. As a quick aside, since there are a variable number of entries for the `interests` list, this suggests that when we ask the customer for their interests, we're going to write some sort of loop asking for more interests until they've indicated that they've finished somehow - perhaps by entering an empty string. We'll deal with this later. In the meantime, leaving out anything to do with films for a moment, the account information could be held in a `list` with 7 elements, the last of which is also a `list` (of interests). As an example of this `list` you could enter the following directly into Python.

Interactive Session

```
>>> A = ['pwilliams','Password1','Peter Williams', '26 High Street,
Kensington, SW10 3ET', '14-01-1993','M', ['films','tv','music']]
```

This looks like a good place to start. We've got a `list` holding 7 items of data, the last of which is also a `list`. Getting at any individual piece of data is simple using an index. Recall that Python starts counting from 0 rather than 1 which means that in the case of this example, `A[0]` will give us `'pwilliams'` whilst `A[6]` will give us `['films','tv','music']`.

This means that it's pretty easy to hold customer information in a single list of 7 entries, with the seventh entry itself a list. But, what about the films?

We could use a `list` structure to hold film information, but each film needs to keep track of its genre and some other information that item 4 asks for, plus we need to keep track of our 'likes'. To try to give us a clear picture of what we're trying to achieve, let's assume that for every film we're going to keep track of its *name*, its *genre*, leading *actors/actresses*, *director* and whether we *like* it. We could store this information in its own `list`, an example of what we might have is shown below.

Interactive Session

```
>>> A = ["Avatar", ["sci-fi","action"], ["Sam Worthington", "Sigourney
Weaver", "Zoe Saldana'"], "James Cameron","Y"]
```

As you can see, the first item in our `list` is the name, in this case `Avatar`, its genre, `[sci-fi, action]` which we've put into a list because it's perfectly possible for a film to be in two or more genres. The third item holds leading actors and/or actresses. Here we've given three in a `list` of its own. The fourth holds the name of the director, in this case, `James Cameron` and finally, the fifth item will hold whether we like it or not, in this case `Y`. If we adopt this structure, each film would have a `list` of its own with 5 entries, the second and third of which is itself a `list`.

Since we're going to hold data on up to 10 films for each customer, we're going to need a list containing up to 10 lists, one for each film. We can add this list of lists to our customer list as its last field, i.e. field 8. It sounds complicated but unfortunately there's no avoiding it if we want to do this scenario properly.

What will this last field look like? If we had three films the last entry in our customer list would look like the following. We've given this list a name, `filmList` so that you can type it into your python shell and then check that you can access each of its fields in the examples that we show shortly.

Interactive Session

```
>>> filmList = [["Avatar",["sci-fi","action"],["Sam Worthington",
"Sigourney Weaver","Zoe Saldana"],"James Cameron","Y"],
["Guardians of the Galaxy",["sci-fi"],["Chris Pratt","James Gunn",
"Vin Diesel","Zoe Saldana"],"James Gunn","Y"],
["Pirates of the Caribbean:The curse of the Black Pearl",
["action","comedy"],["Johnny Depp","Orlando Bloom","Keira
Knightley"],"Gore Verbinski","Y"]]
```

We can access each of the items in `filmList` very easily using an index notation.

Interactive Session

```
>>> filmList[0]
['Avatar', ['sci-fi', 'action'], ['Sam Worthington', 'Sigourney Weaver',
'Zoe Saldana'], 'James Cameron', 'Y']
>>> filmList[1]
['Guardians of the Galaxy', ['sci-fi'], ['Chris Pratt', 'James Gunn',
'Vin Diesel', 'Zoe Saldana'], 'James Gunn', 'Y']
>>> filmList[2]
['Pirates of the Caribbean:The curse of the Black Pearl', ['action',
'comedy'], ['Johnny Depp', 'Orlando Bloom', 'Keira Knoghtley'],
'Gore Verbinski', 'Y']
>>> filmList[0][0]
'Avatar'
>>> filmList[1][0]
'Guardians of the Galaxy'
>>> filmList[2][0]
'Pirates of the Caribbean:The curse of the Black Pearl'
>>> filmList[0][1]
['sci-fi', 'action']
>>> filmList[0][1][0]
'sci-fi'
```

Putting all of this together, let's create a `list` of customers which for want of a better name, we're going to call `Customers` - note that this is plural and starts with a capital letter. A `customer` (singular, lower case letter) is a `list` with 8 fields which will be found in the order shown.

- username, e.g. `pwilliams`
- password, .e.g. `Password1`
- name, e.g. `Peter Williams`
- address, e.g. `26 High Street, Kensington, SW10 3ET`
- date of birth, e.g. `14-01-1993`
- gender, e.g. `M`
- interests, e.g. `['films','tv','music']`
- films watched, e.g. `[['Avatar',['sci-fi'],...`

With this information, `Customers[0]` will hold all of the data relevant to the first customer. To make this a little clearer here is an example of `Customers` which is holding 2 customers, each of which has watched 3 films. The requirement specification asks us to hold data on 10 films for each customer. 3 films are sufficient to show you what is going on here, 10 would obscure matters even further.

Interactive Session

```
>>> Customers = [["pwilliams", "Password1", "Peter Williams",
"26 High Street, Kensington, SW10 3ET", "14-01-1993", "M",
["films","tv","music"],[["Avatar", ["sci-fi","action"], ["Sam Worthington",
"Sigourney Weaver", "Zoe Saldana"], "James Cameron", "Y"],
["Guardians of the Galaxy", ["sci-fi","comedy"], ["Chris Pratt", "James
Gunn","Vin Diesel", "Zoe Saldana"], "James Gunn", "Y"],
["Fargo", ["black comedy", "drama"], ["Frances McDormand", "Steve
Buscemi","William H Macy"], "Joel Coen", "N"]]],
["athos", "P576swwd", "Tom Sawyer", "11 Trim Street, Kensington,
SW10 2TY", "15-12-1987", "M", ["movies","running","squash"],
[["Taxi Driver", ["drama"], ["Robert De Niro", "Jodie Foster", "Cybill
Shepherd"], "Martin Scorsese", "Y"],["The Wizard of Oz", ["musical",
"fantasy", "family"], ["Judy Garland", "Frank Morgan", "Ray Bolger"],
"Victor Fleming", "N"],["Some Like It Hot", ["comedy"], ["Marilyn Monroe",
"Tony Curtis", "Jack Lemmon"], "Billy Wilder", "N"]]]]
```

With this customer list, `Customers[0]` gives us the complete details of our first customer,

Interactive Session

```
>>> Customers[0]
['pwilliams', 'Password1', 'Peter Williams', '26 High Street, Kensington,
SW10 3ET', "14-01-1993'", 'M', ['films', 'tv', 'music'], [['Avatar', ['sci-fi',
'action'], ['Sam Worthington', 'Sigourney Weaver', 'Zoe Saldana'],
'James Cameron', 'Y'], ['Guardians of the Galaxy', ['sci-fi', 'comedy'],
```

```
['Chris Pratt', 'James Gunn', 'Vin Diesel', 'Zoe Saldana'], 'James Gunn',
'Y'], ['Fargo', ['black comedy', 'drama'], ['Frances McDormand',
'Steve Buscemi', 'William H Macy'], 'Joel Coen', 'N']]]
```

while `Customers[0][2]` gives us his full name.

Interactive Session

```
>>> Customers[0][2]
'Peter Williams'
```

If we go further into this nested structure we can get a list of the interests of our second customer by asking for `Customers[1][6]`,

Interactive Session

```
>>> Customers[1][6]
['movies', 'running', 'squash']
```

whilst `Customers[1][6][1]` gives us the second of his interests.

Interactive Session

```
>>> Customers[1][6][1]
'running'
```

If we move on to the eighth field, i.e. `Customers[1][7]`, we'll get the list of films that Tom Sawyer has watched.

Interactive Session

```
>>> Customers[1][7]
[['Taxi Driver', ['drama'], ['Robert De Niro', 'Jodie Foster', 'Cybill
Shepherd'], 'Martin Scorsese', 'Y'], ['The Wizard of Oz', ['musical',
'fantasy', 'family'], ['Judy Garland', 'Frank Morgan', 'Ray Bolger'],
'Victor Fleming', 'N'], ['Some Like It Hot', ['comedy'], ['Marilyn
Monroe', 'Tony Curtis', 'Jack Lemmon'], 'Billy Wilder', 'N']]
```

`Customers[1][7][0]` gives us all the details on his first film.

Interactive Session

```
>>> Customers[1][7][0]
['Taxi Driver', ['drama'], ['Robert De Niro', 'Jodie Foster', 'Cybill
Shepherd'], 'Martin Scorsese', 'Y']
```

To get at its name we'll need to add yet another index. Its name is the first field, so is at position 0. Consequently, `Customers[1][7][0][0]` will give us the name of the first film that Tom Sawyer has watched.

Interactive Session

```
>>> Customers[1][7][0][0]
'Taxi Driver'
```

The genres are in the second field of each film, so to get at the list of genres of Tom Sawyer's second film we'll need `Customers[1][7][1][1]`

Interactive Session

```
>>> Customers[1][7][1][1]
['musical', 'fantasy', 'family']
```

and if we wanted to know how many entries there were in the genre for Tom's second film, `len(Customers[1][7][1][1])` will tell us, and in this case it's 3.

I know that all of this sounds terribly complicated, but if you enter our example `Customers` list you can follow along and try other indices as well. We strongly recommend playing with data structures like this until you are completely familiar with them.

In simple terms, `Customers` is a `list` of customers. Each `customer` is a `list` of 8 fields, the first of which is the username, the second is the password and the last field holds a list of up to 10 films that the customer has watched. Each film is itself a `list` containing the name of the film, it's genre, list of actors, director and whether the customer liked it. To get at any element in this list we simply have to apply the appropriate sequence of indices where reading from left to right, the first number tells us which customer we're looking at. The second number tells us which field we're looking at for that particular customer and further indices allow us to pull out our customer's list of films, names and so on. To solve this particular problem this data structure is absolutely vital and will lie at the heart of pretty much all of the code that we're going to write.

Finally, the scenario wants us to suggest some recommendations for films that our customer might like based on the data gathered. This suggests that we need yet another data structure to hold data on a list of films. As always, this will probably be a `list` but what fields are we going to need?

Since our the list of films in our `customer` list keeps track of the name of the film, its director, like or dislike, some leading actors and actresses and the genre, the last two of which are both `lists` in their own right we're going to have to keep track of at least the same information with the exception of like/dislike, but this time it's not associated with any particular customer, it's merely a list of films. An example of what this data structure might look like is shown below.

Interactive Session

```
>>> Films = [["Avatar",["sci-fi","comedy"],["Sam Worthington",
"Sigourney Weaver", "Zoe Saldana"],"James Cameron"],
["Guardians of the Galaxy",["sci-fi"],["Chris Pratt","James Gunn",
"Vin Diesel","Zoe Saldana"],"James Gunn"],
```

```
["Pirates of the Caribbean:The curse of the Black Pearl",
["action","comedy"],["Johnny Depp","Orlando Bloom", "Keira Knightley"],
"Gore Verbinski"]]
```

In other words, it has exactly the same structure as the list of films in our customer list but **without** the last field for liking or disliking a film. In order to test our code properly, we're going to have to make up a reasonably extensive list of films to use in this project. We've trawled the bowels of `www.imdb.com` to construct a list of 30 recommended films to have something to play with. Rather than force you to enter all of this data yourself, we've saved this list and an example customer list with two customers in two files *films.pkl* and *customers.pkl* which you'll find on our website.

For those of you who'd like to see what the list looks like, the full list of films and customer information are given in the Appendix.

We do appreciate that we've not yet written a single line of code. Instead we've been thinking about our data structures. You might feel that we could have worked all of this out whilst writing code. As previously mentioned, very little of the time spent by professional programmers is actually spent coding; the overwhelming majority of time is spent thinking. Coding is the way that we put all of that thinking to work - to do something useful. It's far more efficient to think things through carefully first rather than rushing in and make things up as we go along.

Having established exactly what our data fields for both our customers and our 30 films are going to look like, we're now at the point where we're ready to think about writing some code. Whereas in the first, much simpler problem, the data file was sufficiently simple to allow us to make a CSV file, when data structures have lists inside of lists which themselves are inside lists we need to use something more complex. Python has a mechanism to save and load (officially called serialize and de-serialize) all sorts of different types of structure. This is called *pickling* and to make use of it you'll need to load the pickle library using the `import pickle` statement. `pickle` has two main methods that you can use, one to `dump` the data to a file and another, `load` to reverse the process and load the data into a new data structure. We've used a text editor to create 30+ films and some customers which we've dumped to `films.pkl` and `customers.pkl` respectively. This particular problem doesn't require you to save film information so you won't need to use `pickle.dump` but you will need to use `pickle.load` to load our files. Since we're going to use this data extensively to test the code that we write, as a first step, let's write a function to load these two files.

We'll start by creating two empty lists. The function will attempt to load the two files, filling the two lists with data if it succeeds. We'll return both lists to the main code. The main code will check to see if either or both of the returned lists are empty and print an appropriate message. If both or neither are empty we'll make use of the `displayList` function that we wrote for our first problem to display what we've loaded.

Note that as we mentioned earlier, we'll need to import the pickle library before trying to load the pickle files. The pseudo code looks like this.

PseudoCode 5.1 Load Pickle File

Require: *filename*

```
procedure LOAD PICKLE FILE
    Try to open filename
    if this fails then
        Print a message to say 'Failed to load filename'
        return an empty list
    else
        Load file contents into contents
        Close file
        return contents
    end if
end procedure
```

This translates pretty directly into code that loads the two pickle files and displays them using the function `displayList` that we wrote in the first sample.

Listing 5.1: Load film and customer information (loadPickleFile.py)

```
import pickle

def displayList(L):
  if L != []:
    for s in L:
      print (s)
  else:
    print("List is empty")

def loadPickleFile(filename):
  try:
    f = open(filename, 'rb')

  except IOError as e:
    print("Failed to open %s" %filename)
    return []

  else:
    content = pickle.load(f)
    f.close()
    return content

# main code starts here
print ("--- Films ---")
```

```
Films = loadPickleFile('films.pkl')
displayList(Films)

print ("--- Customers ---")
Customers = loadPickleFile('customers.pkl')
displayList(Customers)
```

You should run this program and if you've downloaded our pickle files, you'll see 30 films listed followed by two customers. Each customer has watched three films.

This program exits immediately after showing us what it found, but before it did so it loaded 30 example films and a small customer file holding two customers into two complex list structures, `Films` and `Customers` which we can now start to make use of. The next step is to think carefully about what code we're going to write using these data structures to solve the problems posed by the scenario.

5.2 Now what?

Now that we have our data structures sorted and we're clear how to access all parts of the customer and film data structures, we can crack on with solving the actual scenario.

To start with we have to write code to allow a customer to create an account. Each customer account must create a *username* and *password* which has to be secure, i.e. with at least one number and a capital letter. Each customer has to give their *name*, *address*, *date of birth*, *gender*, *interests* together with details on the last ten films that they've watched.

Let's start the ball rolling by asking them for a username and a secure password. Asking for a username is pretty trivial but we also need need to write some code to confirm that the password is secure. According to the brief that we've been given, a password is secure if it contains at least one capital letter and at least one number. This implies that a password of `A1` would be fine but something far more complex like `ComplexPa$$wrd` wouldn't be, since it doesn't contain a number. We've not been asked to check that our password has a minimum length so if we're given something as simple as `A1`, it should be accepted as secure.

Since we need a password from our user and since it has to be secure it makes sense to wait indefinitely for the user to give us something that we can use. This suggests that we create two functions, the first of which, say `getPassword` is called by the main code. It starts a `while` loop within which it asks the user for a password and then makes a call to `secure`. If `secure` returns `True` we can return the password to the main code. If not, we'll stay inside the `while` loop and ask again.

Here's some pseudo-code for the sort of thing we have in mind.

PseudoCode 5.2 Get Username and Password

```
procedure SECURE(password)
    if password is secure then
        return True
    else
        return False
    end if
end procedure

procedure GETPASSWORD
    while True do
        Ask the user for a password
        if SECURE(password) then
            return password
        end if
    end while
end procedure

Ask the user for a username
Call GETPASSWORD and print the result
```

You might be wondering why we haven't created a separate function to ask for the username. The simple reason is that we don't need one. The task is clearly happy to accept anything as a username, whereas we've got more work to do to check that the password is secure. You might also be wondering why we're writing two functions, `getPassword` and `secure`. Why not simply write `getPassword` and stay inside that function until we've checked that it's secure. The answer is that we might have to ask the user for a password quite a few times before they give us something that is secure. More importantly, structurally it's cleaner to have a separate function `secure` which checks the password it's been given rather than try to incorporate asking for a password and checking that it's secure in the same function. It's an important point of programming style that functions should do one job and only one job. Functions are much easier to test if they only do one thing and in this case the job of `getPassword` is to return a password while the job of `secure` is to make sure that it is secure. Each function performs one job and only one job.

Secure passwords must include one or more numbers and one or more capital letters. This implies that whatever password `secure` is given, should first be checked that it includes at least one number and if it does then we should check to see if it also includes at least one capital letter. If it passes both tests we'll return `True`, otherwise we'll have to return `False`.

Bearing this in mind, the pseudo code for the `secure` function would look like this.

PseudoCode 5.3 Check for secure password

Require: *password*

procedure SECURE
    if *password* includes a number **then**
        Set a flag to indicate that we've got a number
    end if
    if *password* includes a capital letter **then**
        Set a flag to indicate that we've got a letter
    end if
    if both flags are True **then**
        return True
    else
        return False
    end if
end procedure

This translates quickly and easily into a short working program as shown in listing 5.2.

Listing 5.2: Get username and secure password (secure.py)

```
def secure(password):
  nums = set('0123456789')
  caps = set('ABCDEFGHIJKLMNOPQRSTUVWXYZ')
  foundNumber = False
  foundCaps = False

  for n in password:
    if (n in nums):
      foundNumber = True
    if (n in caps):
      foundCaps = True

  if foundNumber and foundCaps:
    return True
  else:
    return False

def getPassword():
  while True:
    password = input('Enter Password : ')
    if secure(password):
      return password
    else:
      print("%s must contain at least one number and one capital letter" %(passwor

# main code starts here
username = input('Enter username : ')
```

```
password = getPassword()
print ("Username %s has password %s." %(username, password))
```

We can check that we have at least one number by creating a set of numbers called `nums` and then checking that at least one number in that set can be found in the password using the Python expression `any((n in nums) for n in password)`. We can do exactly the same thing for capital letters. Note that since we need our password to have at least one number *and* it must also have at least one capital letter we ran through `password` twice setting a flag to show that we found a number and a second flag if we found a capital letter. Only if both flags were `True` do we return `True` to `getPassword`.

You should spend some time checking that this function works correctly by passing it different combinations of characters, some including capital letters but no numbers, others numbers but no capital letters and others with both or none.

We got the following output when we ran `secure.py` changing our input each time.

Program Output

```
Enter username : fred
Enter Password : abcd
abcd must contain at least one number and one capital letter
Enter Password : abcd1
abcd1 must contain at least one number and one capital letter
Enter Password : Abcd1
Username fred has password Abcd1.
```

Now that we've got that out of the way, we can move on and get the rest of the data for the account. We aren't asked to validate anything else we ask for so we'll write a simple function to get all of the account information. We'll call it `setupAccount` and in the function we'll ask for the username and password using the code we've already written and that we know works correctly. We'll also ask for the rest of the information, i.e. *name, address, date of birth, gender* and *interests*. In the case of interests we'll have to loop around asking for interests until the user has entered all of them. We'll need to detect when this happens, so we'll assume that there are no more interests if the user enters an empty string by simply hitting the `Enter` key without having entered any text.

We'll start the function by creating an empty `list` called `account`. We'll ask the user for a username which we'll append to `account`. We'll ask for a secure password which we'll also append to `account`. We'll continue by asking the user for their name, address, date of birth and gender, in each case appending their reply to `account`. Finally we'll create an empty `list` called `interests`. We'll set a *flag* called `moreInterests` which we'll initially set to `True` and we'll loop around inside a `while` loop, gathering interests until the user presses `Enter` without entering any text. At which point we'll set `moreInterests` to `False` which will drop us out of the loop next time around. We'll append `interests` to `account` and return `account` to the main code.

The pseudo-code for this function would look something like this.

PseudoCode 5.4 Setup account

```
procedure SETUP ACCOUNT
    Create an empty list called account
    Ask for username and append username to account
    Ask for secure password and append password to account
    Ask for name and append name to account
    Ask for address and append address to account
    Ask for date of birth and append date of birth to account
    Ask for gender and append gender to account

    Create a new list called interests
    Set moreInterests to True
    while moreInterests is True do
        Ask for interest
        if interest is an empty string then
            Set moreInterests to False
        else
            Append interest to interests
        end if
    end while

    Append interests to account
    return account
end procedure
```

This translates to the following code. As with most of our code examples in this book although small, they are complete programs. In this particular case we'll need to add the code for **getPassword** and **secure** for it to run correctly which makes it look bigger than it would otherwise. Concentrate on the code of **setupAccount** and see how closely it resembles our pseudo code.

Listing 5.3: Set up account information (setupAccount.py)

```
def secure(password):
  nums = set('0123456789')
  caps = set('ABCDEFGHIJKLMNOPQRSTUVWXYZ')
  foundNumber = False
  foundCaps = False

  for n in password:
    if (n in nums):
      foundNumber = True
    if (n in caps):
      foundCaps = True

```

```
  if foundNumber and foundCaps:
    return True
  else:
    return False

def getPassword():
  while True:
    password = input('Enter Password : ')
    if secure(password):
      return password
    else:
      print("%s must contain at least one number and one capital letter" %(password))

def setupAccount():
  account = []
  username = input ('Username : ')
  account.append(username)
  password = getPassword()
  account.append(password)
  name = input('Name : ')
  account.append(name)
  address = input('Address : ')
  account.append(address)
  dob = input('Date of Birth [dd-mm-yyyy] : ')
  account.append(dob)
  gender = input('Gender M/F : ')
  account.append(gender)

  interests = []
  moreInterests = True
  while moreInterests:
    interest = input('Interests, empty string to quit : ')
    if interest == "":
      moreInterests = False
    else:
      interests.append(interest)

  account.append(interests)
  return account

# main code starts here
Account = setupAccount()
print(Account)
```

So far, so good. We've written code to allow a user to set up an account which includes a username and secure password. It also includes other information such as name, address and so on. We've saved all of this information in a **list** in which the last element is a list of the user's interests. The following is an example of the output from the program above.

Program Output
```
Username : albert
Enter Password : Abcd1234
Name : Albert Williams
Address : 413 Home Run, London, W3
Date of Birth [dd-mm-yyyy] : 12-12-2002
Gender M/F : M
Interests, empty string to quit : guitar
Interests, empty string to quit : music
Interests, empty string to quit : friends
Interests, empty string to quit :
['albert', 'Abcd1234', 'Albert Williams', '413 Home Run, London, W3',
'12-12-2002', 'M', ['guitar', 'music', 'friends']]
```

What we've still not done however is to ask our user, in this case, Albert for a list of the last 10 films that he's watched. We'll also need to ask him for some information about the film, including genre. The task wants us to *choose additional viewing information other than genre* which we've decided will include names of actors and actresses and director. This means that we'll have to enter all of this information for each of 10 films. We started this project by looking at the data structure that we're going to use in some detail so let's recap.

Each film will hold details of its name, its genre (which will be a list in its own right), its actors and actresses (another list), its director (a single element) and whether or not Albert has `liked` the film, We're going to hold 10 films. We'll build this list of lists by asking Albert for the information and we'll store it as the last element in the `Accounts` list after the list of interests.

This sounds much more complicated than it actually is. Let's break it down by first looking at a function that will let us ask the customer for the details on a single film. When we've written and tested this we can write a second function that can loop around 10 times calling our single film function.

What will this function do? Let's start by giving it a name. Since we're going to ask for data on a single film, let's call it `getSingleFilm`. We're going to have to ask the customer for the name of the film (a single string), the genres (a `list`, leading actors/actresses, (a `list`), its director (a single string) and whether the customer liked the film or not (a single string). Asking for single strings is simple; we can simply use the `input` statement. Asking the customer to enter a list of items suggests some form of loop. We can use exactly the same technique we used earlier to get the `interests` from the customer. In each case, we'll create an empty list, we'll set a flag to `True` and we'll loop around getting new input until the customer hits `Enter` without entering any text at which point we'll set the flag to `False`, thus dropping out of the loop.

We'll start off by creating an empty list which we'll call `film`. We'll then simply ask the user for the relevant information, each of which we'll append to `film` in turn including the list of genres and the list of actors/actresses. The pseudo code is very similar to getting the account information and will look like this.

PseudoCode 5.5 Get Single Film Information

```
procedure GET SINGLE FILM
    Create an empty list called film
    Ask for the film name
    Append the name to film

    Create a new list called genres
    Set the flag moreGenres to True
    while moreGenres is True do
        Ask for a genre
        if we're given an empty string then
            Set moreGenres to False
        else
            Append genre to genres
        end if
    end while
    Append genres to film

    Create a new list called actors
    Set the flag moreActors to True
    while moreActors is True do
        Ask for an actor
        if we're given an empty string then
            Set moreActors to False
        else
            Append actor to actors
        end if
    end while
    Append actors to film

    Ask for the director's name
    Append the name to film

    Ask the user if they liked the film
    Append the result to film
    return film
end procedure
```

Let's write a small program simply to get the information on a single film. We'll add some more code later to ask for more films which we can then append to `Account`.

Listing 5.4: Create a single film (getSingleFilm.py)

```
def getSingleFilm():
  film = []
  name = input('Film name : ')
  film.append(name)

  genres = []
  moreGenres = True
  while moreGenres:
    genre = input('Genre (terminate entries by hitting Enter on its own) : ')
    if genre == "":
      moreGenres = False
    else:
      genres.append(genre)
  film.append(genres)

  actors = []
  moreActors = True
  while moreActors:
    actor = input('Actor (terminate entries by hitting Enter on its own) : ')
    if actor == "":
      moreActors = False
    else:
      actors.append(actor)
  film.append(actors)

  director = input('Director : ')
  film.append(director)

  like = input('Like (Y/N) : ')
  film.append(like)
  return film

# main code starts here
Film = getSingleFilm()
print (Film)
```

We ran the program and got the following output.

Program Output

```
Film name : Aviator
Genre (terminate entries by hitting Enter on its own) : comedy
Genre (terminate entries by hitting Enter on its own) : action
Genre (terminate entries by hitting Enter on its own) : adventure
Genre (terminate entries by hitting Enter on its own) :
Actor (terminate entries by hitting Enter on its own) : Sigourney Weaver
Actor (terminate entries by hitting Enter on its own) : Tom Cruise
Actor (terminate entries by hitting Enter on its own) :
```

```
Director : Lee Chapman
Like (Y/N) : Y
['Aviator', ['comedy', 'action', 'adventure'], ['Sigourney Weaver',
'Tom Cruise'], 'Lee Chapman', 'Y']
```

Now that we have a function which will let us enter details about one film, let's write a new function **getNFilms** which loops around N times getting information about a single film which it will store in a list. The function will take a single parameter, i.e. the number of films N that we want the customer to give us. The pseudo code below shows what we mean.

PseudoCode 5.6 Get N Films

Require: Number of films N

procedure GET N FILMS
  Create an empty list called $films$
  for $i = 1 \rightarrow N$ **do**
    Call getSingleFilm which returns a single list: we'll call it $film$
    Append $film$ to $films$
  end for
  return $films$
end procedure

We can turn this into a working program quite easily. The task wants us to add 10 films for each customer, but that means an awful lot of typing on our behalf. We'll show that everything works correctly by asking for 2, which is much quicker to test.

Listing 5.5: Get N films (getNFilms.py)

```
def getSingleFilm():
  film = []
  name = input('Film name : ')
  film.append(name)

  genres = []
  moreGenres = True
  while moreGenres:
    genre = input('Genre (terminate entries by hitting Enter on its own) : ')
    if genre == "":
      moreGenres = False
    else:
      genres.append(genre)
  film.append(genres)

  actors = []
  moreActors = True
  while moreActors:
```

```
    actor = input('Actor (terminate entries by hitting Enter on its own) : ')
    if actor == "":
      moreActors = False
    else:
      actors.append(actor)
  film.append(actors)

  director = input('Director : ')
  film.append(director)

  like = input('Like (Y/N) : ')
  film.append(like)
  return film

def getNFilms(n):
  films = []
  for _ in range(n):
    film = getSingleFilm()
    films.append(film)
  return films

# main code starts here
Films = getNFilms(2)
print (Films)
```

When we ran this we got the following output.

Program Output

```
Film name : Aviator
Genre (terminate entries by hitting Enter on its own) : action
Genre (terminate entries by hitting Enter on its own) : sci-fi
Genre (terminate entries by hitting Enter on its own) :
Actor (terminate entries by hitting Enter on its own) : Sigourney Weaver
Actor (terminate entries by hitting Enter on its own) : Tom Cruise
Actor (terminate entries by hitting Enter on its own) :
Director : ee Chapman
Like (Y/N) : Y
Film name : The Blues Brothers
Genre (terminate entries by hitting Enter on its own) : comedy
Genre (terminate entries by hitting Enter on its own) : black comedy
Genre (terminate entries by hitting Enter on its own) :
Actor (terminate entries by hitting Enter on its own) : John Belushi
Actor (terminate entries by hitting Enter on its own) : Albert Throgmorton
Actor (terminate entries by hitting Enter on its own) :
Director : Tom Piper
Like (Y/N) : Y
[['Aviator', ['action', 'sci-fi'], ['Sigourney Weaver', 'Tom Cruise'],
'Lee Chapman', 'Y'], ['The Blues Brothers', ['comedy', 'black comedy'],
['John Belushi', 'Albert Throgmorton'], 'Tom Piper', 'Y']]
```

Finally we can put all the pieces together to get all the details for a particular customer. We'll create a new function called `createCustomer` which will begin by calling `setupAccount` to get the username, password, name and so on, which will be returned as a newly created list. It will then call `getNFilms` which in turn calls `getSingleFilm` N times to get a list of films which will be appended to the list returned by `setupAccount`. The following pseudo code shows what we mean.

PseudoCode 5.7 Create Customer

procedure CREATE CUSTOMER
  Call setupAccount, saving the returned list in *customer*
  Call getNFilms and append the returned list to *customer*
  return *customer*
end procedure

We'll put this function into a working program that will create a new `list` containing information on 1 customer, who has entered data on 2 films. If you want to create more customers, each watching 10 films as required by the task, simply change line 102 to 10 and line 101 to whatever number of customers you want to create, but be warned - it is **extremely** tedious entering large amounts of information this way.

The main code starts out by creating an empty `list` called `Customers`. It'll then run through a `for` loop, in this case only once, calling `createCustomer` and appending the `list` that's returned to `Customers`. The code is shown below.

Listing 5.6: Create a customer (createCustomer.py)

```
1  def secure(password):
2    nums = set('0123456789')
3    caps = set('ABCDEFGHIJKLMNOPQRSTUVWXYZ')
4    foundNumber = False
5    foundCaps = False
6
7    for n in password:
8      if (n in nums):
9        foundNumber = True
10     if (n in caps):
11       foundCaps = True
12
13   if foundNumber and foundCaps:
14     return True
15   else:
16     return False
17
18 def getPassword():
19   while True:
```

```
    password = input('Enter Password : ')
    if secure(password):
      return password
    else:
      print("%s must contain at least one number and one capital letter" %(passwor

def setupAccount():
  account = []
  username = input ('Username : ')
  account.append(username)
  password = getPassword()
  account.append(password)
  name = input('Name : ')
  account.append(name)
  address = input('Address : ')
  account.append(address)
  dob = input('Date of Birth [dd-mm-yyyy] : ')
  account.append(dob)
  gender = input('Gender M/F : ')
  account.append(gender)

  interests = []
  moreInterests = True
  while moreInterests:
    interest = input('Interests, empty string to quit : ')
    if interest == "":
      moreInterests = False
    else:
      interests.append(interest)

  account.append(interests)
  return account

def getSingleFilm():
  film = []
  name = input('Film name : ')
  film.append(name)

  genres = []
  moreGenres = True
  while moreGenres:
    genre = input('Genre (terminate entries by hitting Enter on its own) : ')
    if genre == "":
      moreGenres = False
    else:
      genres.append(genre)
  film.append(genres)

  actors = []
```

```
  moreActors = True
  while moreActors:
    actor = input('Actor (terminate entries by hitting Enter on its own) : ')
    if actor == "":
      moreActors = False
    else:
      actors.append(actor)
  film.append(actors)

  director = input('Director : ')
  film.append(director)

  like = input('Like (Y/N) : ')
  film.append(like)
  return film

def getNFilms(n):
  films = []
  for _ in range(n):
    film = getSingleFilm()
    films.append(film)
  return films

def createCustomer(n):
  customer = setupAccount()
  films = getNFilms(n)
  customer.append(films)
  return customer

# main code starts here
# let's create one customers who is required to enter 2 films
Customers = []
for _ in range(1):
  customer = createCustomer(2)
  Customers.append(customer)

print (Customers)
```

Notice that we've passed the number of films we want each customer to choose in the call to **createCustomer**. This is then passed through to **getNFilms** which loops around that number of times calling **getSingleFilm** each time. We've done it like this because it keeps things neat and tidy. The task wants us to create 10 films for each customer. That's extremely tedious so we want a smaller number and although not ideal, passing the number of films that we want into the **createCustomer** function is probably the best way to do this.

The output from running this program looks like this.

Program Output

```
Username : albert
Password (including at least one number and capital letter) : Al123
Name : Albert
Address : 44 Caeffynon, London W12
Date of Birth [dd-mm-yyyy] : 12-12-2002
Gender M/F : M
Interests, empty string to quit : films
Interests, empty string to quit : music
Interests, empty string to quit :
Film name : Housemartin
Genre (terminate entries by hitting Enter on its own) : comedy
Genre (terminate entries by hitting Enter on its own) : action
Genre (terminate entries by hitting Enter on its own) :
Actor (terminate entries by hitting Enter on its own) : Tom Cruise
Actor (terminate entries by hitting Enter on its own) : Alan Rickman
Actor (terminate entries by hitting Enter on its own) :
Director : Lee Chapman
Like (Y/N) : Y
Film name : Bullit
Genre (terminate entries by hitting Enter on its own) : action
Genre (terminate entries by hitting Enter on its own) : war
Genre (terminate entries by hitting Enter on its own) :
Actor (terminate entries by hitting Enter on its own) : Steve McQueen
Actor (terminate entries by hitting Enter on its own) : Robert Vaughan
Actor (terminate entries by hitting Enter on its own) :
Director : Peter Yates
Like (Y/N) : Y
[['albert', 'Al123', 'Albert', '44 Caeffynon', '12-12-2002', 'M',
['films', 'music'], [['Housemartin', ['comedy', 'action'], ['Tom
Cruise', 'Alan Rickman'], 'Lee Chapman', 'Y'], ['Bullit', ['action',
'war'], ['Steve McQueen', 'Robert Vaughan'], 'Peter Yates', Y']]]]
```

5.3 Where are we now

What have we achieved so far? Let's take a look back at the requirement specification. It started off by stating that *When customers sign up they create an account and must enter their details*, such as:

- name ✔
- address ✔
- date of birth ✔
- gender ✔
- interests ✔

We've completed this.

The task then wants us to *Analyse the requirements for this system and design, develop, test and evaluate a program that*

1. enables a customer to set up an account that requires a username and a secure password* to access it. ✔
2. stores the account information and last ten films that the customer has viewed. ✔
3. recommends five films based on the 'genre' of previous viewings**. ✘
4. allows a customer to choose additional viewing preferences other than 'genre'. ✔
5. enables a customer to 'like' a film. ✔
6. uses all of the data gathered to make recommendations for future viewing. ✘

We've completed items 1 and 2 (or at least we will have completed item 2 if we change the range in the code from 2 to 10). We've also allowed the customer to say whether they 'like' a film, i.e. item 5. We've allowed the customer to choose additional viewing preferences, i.e. actors and director. We've not written code to handle items 3 and 6 but our data structures are now in place so that we can complete items 3 and 6 using the information we've gathered from our customer.

We'll start by getting on with item 3. Once recommendations are working by genre it'll be a simple matter to use the two other criteria, i.e. by actor and by director. We'll write a simple interface to allow us to pick whether to make recommendations based on genre, on actors or on director. This will complete the requirements for item 6. Finally, we'll bring everything together in a program using a menu structure much like sample 1 that will do the lot.

Earlier in this section of the book we wrote code that loaded two pickle files, one for customers and one for films. `customer.pkl` holds information on two customers, while `films.pkl` holds details of 30 films. We'll use these two files for testing purposes. Both files are available from our web site, details are in the appendix.

Let's recap and take a look again at the code to load and display the contents of the two pickle files. You can find the code in listing 5.1 on page 73.

This displays the following output (lightly edited to make it easier to read here). The full list of 30 films is in the Appendix.

Program Output

```
--- Films ---
['Avatar', ['sci-fi', 'action'], ['Sam Worthington', 'Sigourney Weaver',
'Zoe Saldana'], 'James Cameron']
['Guardians of the Galaxy', ['sci-fi',`comedy'], ['Chris Pratt',
'James Gunn', 'Vin Diesel', 'Zoe Saldana'], 'James Gunn']
......
......
['The Apartment', ['comedy'], ['Jack Lemmon', 'Shirley MacLaine', 'Fred
MacMurray'], 'Billy Wilder']

--- Customers ---
```

```
['pwilliams', 'Password1', 'Peter Williams', '26 High Street, Kensington,
SW10 3ET', "14-01-1993'", 'M', ['films', 'tv', 'music'],
[['Avatar', ['sci-fi', 'action'], ['Sam Worthington', 'Sigourney Weaver',
'Zoe Saldana'], 'James Cameron', 'Y'],
['Guardians of the Galaxy', ['sci-fi',`comedy'], ['Chris Pratt',
'James Gunn', 'Vin Diesel', 'Zoe Saldana'], 'James Gunn', 'Y'],
['Fargo', ['black comedy', 'drama'], ['Frances McDormand',
'Steve Buscemi', 'William H Macy'], 'Joel Coen',`N']]]

['athos', 'P576swwd', 'Tom Sawyer', '11 Trim Street, Kensington,
SW10 2TY','15-12-1987', 'M', ['movies', 'running', 'squash'],
[['Taxi Driver', ['drama'], ['Robert DeNiro', 'Jodie Foster',
'Cybill Shepherd'], 'Martin Scorsese',`Y'],
['The Wizard of Oz', ['musical', 'fantasy', 'family'], ['Judy Garland',
'Frank Morgan', 'Ray Bolger'], 'Victor Fleming',`N'],
['Some Like It Hot', ['comedy'], ['Marilyn Monroe', 'Tony Curtis',
'Jack Lemmon'], 'Billy Wilder',`N']]]
```

As you can see from the output, we have two customers, one with username `pwilliams` and the other with username `athos`. `pwilliams` has three films listed, `Avatar`, `Guardians of the Galaxy` and `Fargo`. `athos` also has three films listed, `Taxi Driver`, `The Wizard of Oz` and `Some Like it Hot`.

Let's look at what we need to do to make recommendations based on genre.

Our master list is `Customers` which means that our first customer is `Customers[0]`, which in this case is `pwilliams`. The 8th element of each customer, say in the case of `pwilliams`, `Customers[0][7]` will be a list of all the films watched by `pwilliams`. In this case,`Customers[0][7][0]` will refer to the first film in `pwilliams`'s list. Whether `pwilliams` liked this particular film or not is held in the 5th item of the list holding data on each film, i.e. in this case `Customers[0][7][0][4]`. `Avatar` is `pwilliam`'s first film. He liked this film - we know this because `Customers[0][7][0][4]` is holding 'Y', so we should now look at the genre. Since genre is the second item in the list, i.e. `Customers[0][7][0][1]`, we can see that the genres associated with `Avatar` are in this case `['sci-fi', 'action']`.

We can then extract each of the genres in turn from the list of genres associated with `Avatar` that `pwilliams` liked and look in our list of films for the same genres. We could then display every film that matched any of these genres (or as the task wants, at most five).

Essentially for each customer we're going to look at each of the films that they've got listed. For each of these films we'll see if they liked it. If they did, for each entry in the genres that the film has specified we'll try to match that genre with genres in our film list of which we'll print out at most 5.

I know that this sounds complicated but let's look at the pseudo code for this.

PseudoCode 5.8 Match genres

Require: *customer*, *films*

```
procedure MATCH GENRES
    Create an empty list called recommended
    Set counter = 0
    for each film the customer watched do
        if the customer liked the film then
            for each film in the example films list do
                if any genres match then
                    Append the film name to recommended
                    counter = counter + 1
                    if counter > 4 then
                        return recommended
                    end if
                end if
            end for
        end if
    end for
    return recommended
end procedure
```

The task want us to return at most 5 recommended films hence the use of a counter to keep track of how many recommended films we can find based on the genre. What does this look like in code?

Listing 5.7: Match on genre (matchGenres.py)

```
import pickle

def loadPickleFile(filename):
  try:
    f = open(filename, 'rb')

  except IOError as e:
    print("Failed to open %s" %filename)
    return []

  else:
    content = pickle.load(f)
    f.close()
    return content

def matchEachCustomer(customer, films):
  any_in = lambda a,b: any(i in a for i in b)
  recommended = []
  counter = 0
  for film in customer[7]:
```

```
21     if film[4] == 'Y':
22       genres = film[1]
23       for f in films:
24         if any_in(genres, f[1]):
25           recommended.append(f[0])
26           counter = counter + 1
27           if counter > 4:
28             return recommended
29   return recommended
30
31
32 def matchGenre(customers, films):
33   for customer in customers:
34     L = matchEachCustomer(customer, films)
35     print ('Recommended films for ' + customer[2])
36     print (L)
37
38
39 # main code starts here
40 Films = loadPickleFile('films.pkl')
41 Customers = loadPickleFile('customers.pkl')
42 matchGenre(Customers, Films)
```

If you run this program with our pickle files, you'll get the following output.

```
Program Output
Recommended films for Peter Williams
['Avatar', 'Guardians of the Galaxy', 'Pirates of the Caribbean:
The curse of the Black Pearl', 'Gladiator', 'Jaws']
Recommended films for Tom Sawyer
['The Godfather', 'A Woman Under the Influence', 'To Kill a Mockingbird',
'The Godfather: Part II', 'Boogie Nights']
```

The code follows the pseudo code pretty closely. We've added one little nugget, a *lambda* function where we've declared a new function called `any_in` which takes two parameters, in our case lists, and checks to see whether any elements from the first list is present in the second list. `any_in` returns `True` if there are, `False` if not. If we get `True` we can then append the name of the film to our growing list of recommendations. We've split the code into two functions because we want to provide recommendations for each customer. Our pickle file of customers has exactly two customers, `Peter Williams` and `Tom Sawyer`. `matchGenre` is called from the main body of the program and for each customer passes the customer and list of films to `matchEachCustomer` where the match is attempted and a list of recommendations is passed back (if any).

At the sake of explaining stuff that you already know, in line 20, `customer[7]` refers to the 8th field, i.e. the list of films so by writing `for film in customer[7]` we're taking each film in turn from the list of films watched by the `customer` that has been passed to us. For each film, the field with index 4 holds either `Y` or `N` depending on whether the customer liked this particular film. Line 21 is therefore simply checking that the customer liked this particular film. If they did, the genres are held in the second field of the film, i.e. index 1 so `film[1]` is a list of genres for this particular film. Line 23 then iterates through each film one by one in the collection of 30 films that we passed into the function and for each one, line 24 checks to see whether any of the genres in the film that the customer liked matches any of the genres in each of the films in the collection of 30 films. If any do, the name of the film (field 0) is appended to the `recommended` list of films.

The more eagle-eyed amongst you might have noticed that the recommendations for Peter Williams includes two films that he's already watched, i.e. *Avatar* and *Guardians of the Galaxy*. There's nothing in the specification that asks us specifically for films that we've not previously watched, even so we'll make a mental note to deal with it later.

So, that's item 3 in the project's list of requirements covered. Let's move on to covering item 4 which will allow us to recommend films based on other criteria, in our case on actors/actresses and directors.

If you think carefully about this, matching on genre is only done on a one line, line 22, which we use again in line 24 in our small matching function. Otherwise the pseudo code and Python code should be identical. The only difference is in deciding what elements to match against. In the code for matching on genre above we compared the second element, i.e. genre in the customer film section with the second element in our example film list. It is not coincidental that we're matching the second elements in both cases. We set up our data structures so that the film information that we stored for each customer matched the example film list in every position except that we added an additional element in the case of the customer, i.e. whether they liked a film or not. This means that with a very small change to the code we can use exactly the same code to handle our two other criteria. In fact, if we modify our `matchGenre` code so that we pass the index that we want to match against into the function, the same code will work for all three criteria. If we pass in the value 1, we'll match on genre because it's at position 1, i.e. it's the second item in the list. If we pass in the value 2, we'll match on the third item in the list, i.e. actors/actresses and if we pass in the value 3 we'll match on director.

We should also change the name of the function because we're not just matching on genre now. We'll change `matchGenre` to `matchCriteria` and in addition to giving it customer and the list of example films, we'll also give it the index of the element that we want to match against. `matchCriteria` will pass this on to `matchEachCustomer` and we're in business as the following small program shows.

There is one other change that we need to make. Our little function `any_in` takes two parameters, `a` and `b` and checks to see whether anything that is in `a` is also in `b`. This is fine when the `a` and `b` are both lists but if, as is the case with directors these are single strings, `any_in` will look to match characters inside the string which isn't what we want.

There is a simple solution to this. At the start of the function we'll check to see whether we're matching on DIRECTOR and if so we'll set our any_in function to check for equality rather than membership.

Listing 5.8: Match on any criteria (matchCriteria.py)

```
import pickle

# field indices
FILM_NAME = 0
CUSTOMER_NAME = 2

GENRE = 1
ACTOR = 2
DIRECTOR = 3
LIKE = 4
FILMS = 7

def loadPickleFile(filename):
  try:
    f = open(filename, 'rb')

  except IOError as e:
    print("Failed to open %s" %filename)
    return []

  else:
    content = pickle.load(f)
    f.close()
    return content

def matchEachCustomer(customer, films, criteria):
  if criteria == DIRECTOR:
    any_in = lambda a,b: (a == b)
  else:
    any_in = lambda a,b: any(i in a for i in b)

  recommended = []
  counter = 0
  for film in customer[FILMS]:
    if film[LIKE] == 'Y':
      for f in films:
        if any_in(film[criteria], f[criteria]):
          recommended.append(f[FILM_NAME])
          counter = counter + 1
          if counter > 4:
            return recommended
  return recommended

def matchCriteria(customers, films, criteria):
```

```
  for customer in customers:
    L = matchEachCustomer(customer, films, criteria)
    print ('Recommended films for ' + customer[CUSTOMER_NAME])
    print (L)

# main code starts here
Films = loadPickleFile('films.pkl')
Customers = loadPickleFile('customers.pkl')

print('--- Matching on genre ---')
matchCriteria(Customers, Films, GENRE)
print('--- Matching on actors ---')
matchCriteria(Customers, Films, ACTOR)
print('--- Matching on director ---')
matchCriteria(Customers, Films, DIRECTOR)
```

We've taken the opportunity to replace the value of the index numbers that we're interested in with words. Python doesn't have constants as such, but it's still well worth while pretending that it does to make the code a little clearer.

If you run this program you'll get the following output.

Program Output

```
--- Matching on genre ---
Recommended films for Peter Williams
['Avatar', 'Guardians of the Galaxy', 'Pirates of the Caribbean:
The curse of the Black Pearl', 'Gladiator', 'Jaws']
Recommended films for Tom Sawyer
['The Godfather', 'A Woman Under the Influence', 'To Kill a Mockingbird',
'The Godfather: Part II', 'Boogie Nights']
--- Matching on actors ---
Recommended films for Peter Williams
['Avatar', 'Guardians of the Galaxy', 'Avatar', 'Guardians of the Galaxy']
Recommended films for Tom Sawyer
['The Godfather: Part II', 'Taxi Driver', 'Goodfellas', 'Raging Bull']
--- Matching on director ---
Recommended films for Peter Williams
['Avatar', 'Guardians of the Galaxy']
Recommended films for Tom Sawyer
['Taxi Driver', 'Goodfellas']
```

If you look closely at the output you'll see that we're matching correctly depending on the criteria we're using but as mentioned earlier, we're returning films that the customer has already watched and we're also giving the same recommendations more than once for the same criteria. Ideally we should make sure that we're not simply recommending films that we've already watched and we should also remove any duplicates. Let's deal with these one at a time.

Removing films from the recommendation list that we've already watched should be straightforward. Inside `matchEachCustomer`, we could make a list of the names of the films we've already watched and then after we've checked if we liked that film but before we add it to the `recommended` list we could check if the film was one we'd already watched and only add it to the list if we hadn't. That would work.

Regarding the second problem where we repeat our recommendations. That's easily solved by simply checking before we add a film name to `recommended` that it's not already `recommended`. The pseudo code to solve both our problems would be something like the following.

PseudoCode 5.9 Match Criteria

```
Require: customer, films, criteria
procedure MATCH CRITERIA
    Create an empty list called watched
    for each film in our customer's list of films do
        Append the name to watched
    end for

    Create an empty list called recommended
    Set counter = 0
    for each customer do
        for each film that the customer has watched do
            for each film in the example films list do
                if any criteria match then
                    if the film name is not in watched then
                        if the film name is not in recommended then
                            Append the film name to recommended
                            counter = counter + 1
                            if counter > 4 then
                                return recommended
                            end if
                        end if
                    end if
                end if
            end for
        end for
    end for
    return recommended
end procedure
```

The code to handle this is as follows. Note that we've added a print statement to display the contents of `watched`. This reminds us what films each customer has watched as we look at the recommendations.

Listing 5.9: Match (match.py)

```
import pickle

# field index
FILM_NAME = 0
CUSTOMER_NAME = 2

GENRE = 1
ACTOR = 2
DIRECTOR = 3
LIKE = 4
FILMS = 7
NUMBER_OF_FILMS_WANTED = 4

def loadPickleFile(filename):
  try:
    f = open(filename, 'rb')

  except IOError as e:
    print("Failed to open %s" %filename)
    return []

  else:
    content = pickle.load(f)
    f.close()
    return content

def matchEachCustomer(customer, films, criteria):
  if criteria == DIRECTOR:
    any_in = lambda a,b: (a == b)
  else:
    any_in = lambda a,b: any(i in a for i in b)

  watched = []
  for film in customer[FILMS]:
    watched.append(film[FILM_NAME])

  print(str(customer[CUSTOMER_NAME]) + " has watched " + str(watched))

  recommended = []
  counter = 0
  for film in customer[FILMS]:
    if film[LIKE] == 'Y':
      for f in films:
        if any_in(film[criteria], f[criteria]):
          if not f[FILM_NAME] in watched:
            if not f[FILM_NAME] in recommended:
              recommended.append(f[FILM_NAME])
```

```
            counter = counter + 1
            if counter > NUMBER_OF_FILMS_WANTED:
              return recommended
  return recommended


def matchCriteria(customers, films, criteria):
  for customer in customers:
    L = matchEachCustomer(customer, films, criteria)
    print ('Recommended films for ' + customer[CUSTOMER_NAME])
    print (L)

# main code starts here
Films = loadPickleFile('films.pkl')
Customers = loadPickleFile('customers.pkl')

print('--- Matching on genre ---')
matchCriteria(Customers, Films, GENRE)
print('--- Matching on actors ---')
matchCriteria(Customers, Films, ACTOR)
print('--- Matching on director ---')
matchCriteria(Customers, Films, DIRECTOR)
```

When we run this program, we get the following output.

Program Output

```
--- Matching on genre ---
Peter Williams has watched ['Avatar', 'Guardians of the Galaxy', 'Fargo']
Recommended films for Peter Williams
['Pirates of the Caribbean:The curse of the Black Pearl', 'Gladiator', 'Jaws',
'Tootsie', 'Annie Hall']
Tom Sawyer has watched ['Taxi Driver', 'The Wizard of Oz', 'Some Like It Hot']
Recommended films for Tom Sawyer
['The Godfather', 'A Woman Under the Influence', 'To Kill a Mockingbird',
'The Godfather: Part II', 'Boogie Nights']
--- Matching on actors ---
Peter Williams has watched ['Avatar', 'Guardians of the Galaxy', 'Fargo']
Recommended films for Peter Williams
[]
Tom Sawyer has watched ['Taxi Driver', 'The Wizard of Oz', 'Some Like It Hot']
Recommended films for Tom Sawyer
['The Godfather: Part II', 'Goodfellas', 'Raging Bull']
--- Matching on director ---
Peter Williams has watched ['Avatar', 'Guardians of the Galaxy', 'Fargo']
Recommended films for Peter Williams
[]
Tom Sawyer has watched ['Taxi Driver', 'The Wizard of Oz', 'Some Like It Hot']
Recommended films for Tom Sawyer
['Goodfellas']
```

This is much better, no duplicates and no recommendations of films that we've already watched. This looks like we've covered items 3 and 6. We've not been asked to do so, but a nice menu driven interface along the lines of the first sample would tie it all together nicely and give us something neat to play with. The specification doesn't actually ask us to save any customer information and there's nothing about any film collection that we can recommend films from. All of these are additional things that we could add to the code if we wanted.

A final solution incorporating most of these additions is shown below.

Listing 5.10: Complete code - Sample 2 (sample2.py)

```
# sample 2
import pickle

# field index
FILM_NAME = 0
CUSTOMER_NAME = 2

GENRE = 1
ACTOR = 2
DIRECTOR = 3
LIKE = 4
FILMS = 7
NUMBER_OF_FILMS_WANTED = 4

def loadPickleFile(filename):
  try:
    f = open(filename, 'rb')

  except IOError as e:
    print("Failed to open %s" %filename)
    return []

  else:
    content = pickle.load(f)
    f.close()
    return content

def matchEachCustomer(customer, films, criteria):
  if criteria == DIRECTOR:
    any_in = lambda a,b: (a == b)
  else:
    any_in = lambda a,b: any(i in a for i in b)

  watched = []
  for film in customer[FILMS]:
```

```
    watched.append(film[FILM_NAME])

  recommended = []
  counter = 0
  for film in customer[FILMS]:
    if film[LIKE] == 'Y':
      for f in films:
        if any_in(film[criteria], f[criteria]):
          if not f[FILM_NAME] in watched:
            if not f[FILM_NAME] in recommended:
              recommended.append(f[FILM_NAME])
              counter = counter + 1
              if counter > NUMBER_OF_FILMS_WANTED:
                return recommended
  return recommended

def matchCriteria(customers, films, criteria):
  for customer in customers:
    L = matchEachCustomer(customer, films, criteria)
    print ('Recommended films for ' + customer[CUSTOMER_NAME])
    print (L)

def secure(password):
  nums = set('0123456789')
  caps = set('ABCDEFGHIJKLMNOPQRSTUVWXYZ')
  foundNumber = False
  foundCaps = False

  for n in password:
    if (n in nums):
      foundNumber = True
    if (n in caps):
      foundCaps = True

  if foundNumber and foundCaps:
    return True
  else:
    return False

def getPassword():
  while True:
    password = input('Enter Password : ')
    if secure(password):
      return password
    else:
      print("%s must contain at least one number and one capital letter" %(passwor

def setupAccount():
  account = []
```

```
  username = input ('Username : ')
  account.append(username)
  password = getPassword()
  account.append(password)
  name = input('Name : ')
  account.append(name)
  address = input('Address : ')
  account.append(address)
  dob = input('Date of Birth [dd-mm-yyyy] : ')
  account.append(dob)
  gender = input('Gender M/F : ')
  account.append(gender)

  interests = []
  moreInterests = True
  while moreInterests:
    interest = input('Interests, empty string to quit : ')
    if interest == "":
      moreInterests = False
    else:
      interests.append(interest)

  account.append(interests)
  return account

def getSingleFilm():
  film = []
  name = input('Film name : ')
  film.append(name)

  genres = []
  moreGenres = True
  while moreGenres:
    genre = input('Genre (terminate entries by hitting Enter on its own) : ')
    if genre == "":
      moreGenres = False
    else:
      genres.append(genre)
  film.append(genres)

  actors = []
  moreActors = True
  while moreActors:
    actor = input('Actor (terminate entries by hitting Enter on its own) : ')
    if actor == "":
      moreActors = False
    else:
      actors.append(actor)
  film.append(actors)
```

```

  director = input('Director : ')
  film.append(director)

  like = input('Like (Y/N) : ')
  film.append(like)
  return film

def getNFilms(n):
  films = []
  for _ in range(n):
    film = getSingleFilm()
    films.append(film)
  return films

def createCustomer(n):
  customer = setupAccount()
  films = getNFilms(n)
  customer.append(films)
  return customer

def recommend(Customers, Films):
  while True:
    print ('1. Recommend on Genre')
    print ('2. Recommend on actors/actresses')
    print ('3. Recommend on Director')
    print ('4. Main menu')

    option = input('Select an option : ')
    if option == '1':
      print('--- Matching on genre ---')
      matchCriteria(Customers, Films, GENRE)
    elif option == '2':
      print('--- Matching on actors/actresses ---')
      matchCriteria(Customers, Films, ACTOR)
    elif option == '3':
      print('--- Matching on director ---')
      matchCriteria(Customers, Films, DIRECTOR)
    elif option == '4':
      return
    else:
      print ('Not a valid choice - try again')


def mainMenu(Customers, Films):
  while True:
    print ('1. Enter new customer information')
    print ('2. Recommend films')
    print ('3. Logout')
```

```

    option = input('Select an option : ')
    if option == '1':
      customer = createCustomer(2)
      Customers.append(customer)
    elif option == '2':
      recommend(Customers, Films)
    elif option == '3':
      return
    elif option == '0':
      print("--- Customers ---")
      print(Customers)
    else:
      print ('Not a valid choice - try again')

# main code starts here
Films = loadPickleFile('films.pkl')
Customers = loadPickleFile('customers.pkl')
mainMenu(Customers, Films)
```

6

Sample 3

Scenario

Clark is designing a game that allows players to move around a 7x7 grid, each position in the board has a number to represent the space, as shown in Table 6.1.

43	44	45	46	47	48	49
42	41	40	39	38	37	36
29	30	31	32	33	34	35
28	27	26	25	24	23	22
15	16	17	18	19	20	21
14	13	12	11	10	9	8
1	2	3	4	5	6	7

Table 6.1: The board

Players must move through the spaces in numerical order, starting from space 1, all the way to space 49.

Player(s) roll two 6-sided dice and move that number of places, e.g. if they are on space 4 and they roll a 3 and a 2, they move 5 spaces to space 9.

The winner is the first player to reach space 49. Players do not need to roll an exact number to reach space 49, for example if they are on 48 and roll 3, they will still win.

Analyse the requirements for this system and design, develop, test and evaluate a program that:

1. allows 2 players to play the game
2. allows the players to take it in turns to roll two 6 sided dice and move
3. display the result of each move on the board

4. makes a player move back the number of positions rolled if they roll a double (two dice with the same number)
5. displays the messages below when the condition for display is met (the condition is given to you below):

    a) Start Game message: displays either just before the first roll of the dice, or upon start-up
    b) A message when a "double" is rolled (e.g. a 3 on each die): displays only when the score both die are identical
    c) Win message when they finish the game: displays when the player score is 49 or greater

    These messages should be:

    - stored externally and then read in to the game at the start of the program

    Some games have obstacles or challenges that may send you back or forward by a set number of spaces.
6. Create a way of externally storing at least 4 "obstacles" and the number of squares they move forward or backward by.
7. Load these obstacles into the game when it starts.

So, where to start?

Reading through the scenario it's clear that we need to write a game. Furthermore a game with two players, each rolling a 6-sided die and moving along the board from position 1 by adding the value on the two dice to the current position until one player reaches a value that's greater than or equal to 49. We'll have to display the result of each move on a board, presumably just like the one they've shown us. The game is made a little more complex in that the player has to go back the number of spaces given by the two dice if they throw a 'double'. We need to show some messages which are to be stored in a separate file and loaded when the game starts. Finally, we need at least four 'obstacles', which will either add or subtract a given number of squares if the player lands on them. These also need to be stored externally and loaded when the game starts.

That's about it apart from wondering whether the task want us to use physical dice or does it want us to simulate the throws of the dice. It'll actually be much quicker and easier to test that our code works if we use simulated dice. This means that the computer can play both players and run through a game extremely quickly, perhaps printing everything to the screen which we can read through carefully to ensure that all moves and calculations happen correctly. We'll start out using the python random number generator to simulate throwing the dice and we'll change the code to allow two physical dice once we've finished thoroughly testing the program.

In summary.

- Two players, taking it in turn to 'throw' a couple of dice.
- They move a number of squares based on the values of the two dice.
- We need to show the position (on the board) after each move.
- There are at least four 'obstacles'.
- We must give some messages.
- Messages and obstacles are to be stored externally, i.e. in separate files.

- The player that scores 49 or above wins the game.

At first sight it looks like everything revolves around the board which is essentially a list of numbers from 1 to 49. Each player will be somewhere on the board, i.e. each player will hold a number in the range 1 to 49. We're going to assume that both players start at position 1. Notice that it's perfectly possible for a player's position to be negative - for example imagine that the first player throws a double 3 on his first throw - technically he'll have to move to position $1 + (-6) = -5$. Does this mean that if the player on his next move throws another double he or she moves even further into negative number territory? Probably not, so we'll 'clamp' each player to the value 1.

We're going to need to display the board in the format shown to us and we're going to have to indicate somehow the position of each of the players on the board. It's difficult, but not impossible to do this on the command line so this suggests instead that we'll need to produce a graphical program. There are a number of graphics libraries that we might use, but let's park this for the moment. We'll write the program without displaying any sort of board and instead simply concentrate on the functionality of the program. We can easily keep track of where each player is by sending appropriate messages to the screen and it's a lot easier than messing around with graphics for the moment.

So, where shall we start?

6.1 Throwing the dice

Let's begin by thinking of simulating the throw of the dice. It's ambiguously worded but it's probably safe to assume that the task will want us to use real physical dice, but as we said earlier, if we simulate the dice instead we can get the computer to play the game from start to finish in a matter of milliseconds, meanwhile printing out all the calculations its going through. This means that we can read through the messages that it produces to check that our code is working correctly. This means that development will be much, much quicker.

To simulate the throw of a single die we can use the python `random` library which has a `randint(from, to)` function which we can use. By calling `random:randint(1,6)` we'll get back an integer in the range 1 to 6 inclusive which is exactly what we want. Later, when we've finished testing, we can replace the line by an `input()` function and we'll have our physical dice instead.

Our function is going to simulate both dice and will return a value. Inside the function we'll add the values from the two dice together and if both dice give the same value, which we'll call a double, we'll return a negative number instead. The pseudo code for this function is pretty straightforward.

PseudoCode 6.1 Throw 2 dice

procedure THROW DICE
    Get first value, call this $d1$
    Get second value, call this $d2$
    if $d1 = d2$ **then**
        $score = -(d1 + d2)$
    else
        $score = d1 + d2$
    end if
    return $score$
end procedure

This translates almost line for line into python as

Listing 6.1: Throw 2 dice (throwDice.py)

```
import random

def throwDice():
    d1 = random.randint(1,6)
    d2 = random.randint(1,6)

    if d1 == d2:
        score = -(d1+d2)
    else:
        score = d1+d2

    return score

# code starts here
for x in range(6):
  print (throwDice())
```

When you run this you should get six random values in the range -12, (in the case of getting a six on both dice), to 11 (when we must have got a 5 on one die and a 6 on the other).

Now that we've got some simulated dice working, let's add some code for each of the players to take a turn. What do we want `turn` to do?

The whole point of having a turn is to move to a new position on the board, and ultimately try to make it to the end before the other player. This suggests that `turn` should at least be given the player's current position to which it will add the value returned from the `throwDice` function to it. It'll then pass the new position back to the main code. Before it does so however, it makes sense to check the new position and if it's below 1 to set it equal, i.e. clamp it to 1.

This suggests that the pseudo code for the `turn` function should look like this.

PseudoCode 6.2 Take a turn

```
Require: pos                                    ▷ our current position
procedure TURN
    Call throwDice() - it returns val
    newpos = val + pos
    if newpos < 1 then
        newpos = 1
    end if
    return newpos
end procedure
```

We also need to check to see whether a player has won. They will have if their position is equal to or more than 49 after the dice is thrown. The pseudo code for this function is very simple.

PseudoCode 6.3 Check for winner

```
Require: pos                                    ▷ our current position
procedure WINNER
    if pos > 48 then
        return True
    else
        return False
    end if
end procedure
```

These two functions will work but before we write some code to implement this, let's think about the main program that's going to call `turn` and `winner`. Both players' start on the first square, i.e both players start in position 1. Each player will then take it in turns to roll the dice, adjusting their position after each turn. The first player to score 49 or more will win. `turn` will give us back the new position and `winner` will tell us whether a player has scored 49 or more. The only thing that we're interested in about them is their position, so `A` will hold the current position of player A and `B` will hold the current position of player `B`. We could have given them longer names such as `Player_A` and `Player_B`, but although we always like to see good descriptive names used at all times, using `A` and `B` should be clear, it's succinct and it saves lots of typing.

The pseudo code for the main code might look something like this:

PseudoCode 6.4 Main playing code

```
Set A = 1
Set B = 1

while True do
    Give Player A a turn
    if A has won then
        Print a message to say so
        Leave the program
    else
        Give Player B a turn
        if B has won then
            Print a message to say so
            Leave the program
        end if
    end if
end while
```

The corresponding code is pretty close to this.

Listing 6.2: Main code (main.py)

```
from random import *

def throwDice(player):
    d1 = randint(1,6)
    d2 = randint(1,6)
    #d1 = int(input("First dice: "))
    #d2 = int(input("Second dice: "))

    if d1 == d2:
        score = -(d1+d2)
        print (player + ': double ' + str(d1) + ': returns ' + str(score))
    else:
        score = d1+d2
        print (player +' ' +str(d1) + ',' +str(d2) +': returns ' +str(score))
    return score


def turn(position, player):
    position = position + throwDice(player)
    if position < 1:
        position = 1
    return position


def winner(position):
```

```
    if position > 48:
        return True
    else:
        return False


# program starts here
# Players A and B both start in square 1
A = 1
B = 1

while True:
    A = turn(A, "A")
    if winner(A):
        print ('Player A scored ' + str(A) + ', Player A has won')
        break
    else:
        print ('Player A new position: ' + str(A))
        B = turn(B, "B")
        if winner(B):
            print ('Player B scored ' + str(B) + ', Player B has won')
            break
        else:
            print ('Player B new position: ' + str(B))
```

Note that we've passed a string "A" or "B" to **turn** and subsequently to **throwDice** so that we can print a message saying which player is currently having a turn to let us know exactly what is going on.

If you run this you'll get output something like the following. It's very unlikely to be exactly the same because your random number generator will produce different throws for the dice than ours has.

Program Output

```
A 4,3: returns 7
Player A new position: 8
B 5,6: returns 11
Player B new position: 12
A 2,4: returns 6
Player A new position: 14
B 5,2: returns 7
Player B new position: 19
A 4,3: returns 7
Player A new position: 21
B: double 2: returns -4
Player B new position: 15
A: double 5: returns -10
Player A new position: 11
B 3,6: returns 9
```

```
Player B new position: 24
A 5,1: returns 6
Player A new position: 17
B 3,6: returns 9
Player B new position: 33
A 6,1: returns 7
Player A new position: 24
B 6,1: returns 7
Player B new position: 40
A 1,3: returns 4
Player A new position: 28
B 1,5: returns 6
Player B new position: 46
A 3,1: returns 4
Player A new position: 32
B 3,2: returns 5
Player B scored 51, Player B has won
```

If you read through this carefully you'll see that the the scores from the two dice are being added to the current position correctly. The new positions have been adjusted accordingly. The game works. We're not displaying anything on a grid yet, but that's not important at the moment; we will later. As a quick aside, note the two lines of commented out code. If we replaced the two calls to `randint` with the two lines below them, we'd change the game to using physical dice. In the meantime, let's tackle the next problem - obstacles.

6.2 Obstacles

The task wants us to provide at least four obstacles. Obstacles is a little bit of a misnomer because some obstacles will cause us to add a negative value to our current position, taking us closer to 1 whilst others will add a positive value to our position, taking us closer to 49. The only things that matter as far as an obstacle is concerned is its position, i.e. what square it's on and what it's value is. The task wants us to store these values in an external file, which for want of a better name we'll call `obstacles.csv`. Because each obstacle is simply a tuple of two numbers, i.e., position and value, we might as well store our data in a text file, which we can write by hand, separating the values by a comma. Since our data is comma separated, we might as well use the library module `csv` to load `obstacles.csv` saving the values in a `list` of `lists`.

A typical obstacle file will look like the following

```
12,-2
17,3
25,7
33,-6
39,3
```

The first line, representing our first obstacle, tells us that if a player lands on position 12 on the board, a value of -2 should be added to the current position meaning that he or she will have to go back two places to position 10. The second line will add 3 to any player landing at position 17, moving them on to position 20. We've got five lines in our file, i.e. 5 obstacles.

OK. Let's write some code to load the file. We're going to use the library `csv`, each line will be loaded into a `list` consisting of two elements, `[position, value]`. In our example file we've got five lines, so we'll create five lists. It makes sense to put these lists into a `list` called `obstacles`. We're going to `try` to load the file first. If the load operation fails we'll simply return an empty list. If it succeeds, we'll print a message to say so, create an empty list called `obstacles` and read each of the lines into a `list` which we'll append to `obstacles`. We'll return `obstacles` to our calling code and display it, simply to show that we've loaded it correctly. The following pseudo code should make this clear.

PseudoCode 6.5 Load Obstacles File

```
procedure LOAD OBSTACLES FILE
    Try to open the obstacles file
    if loading fails then
        return an empty list
    else
        Create an empty list called obstacles
        for each line in the obstacles file do
            Read the line into a list and append it to obstacles
        end for
        Close the file
        return obstacles
    end if
end procedure
```

This translates directly into code as

Listing 6.3: Load obstacles file (loadObstacles.py)

```
import csv


def loadObstacles():
# start by trying to load our data file.
  try:
    f = open("obstacles.csv", "r")

  except IOError as e:
    return []

```

```
  else:
    print("Obstacles file opened successfully")
    obstacles = []
    for line in csv.reader(f):
      obstacles.append(line)
    f.close()
    return obstacles

# program starts here
L = loadObstacles()
print(L)
```

If you run this with a suitable obstacles file you should see something like this.

```
Program Output
Obstacles file opened successfully
[['12', '-2'], ['17', '3'], ['25', '7'], ['33', '-6'], ['39', '3']]
```

We now have code to load our obstacles and to store them safely in a list of lists called `obstacles`. Now we need to use the information we've loaded to affect the player's progress.

Obstacles are used when a player arrives at the obstacle's position. This suggests that once each player has thrown the dice and calculated their new position, we should call a function, let's call it `checkForObstacles` and we'll give it the new position. `checkForObstacles` should look at the `obstacles` list of lists to see whether the first element of each of its elements is the same as the position it's been given. If so, it should add to the position whatever value is associated with the obstacle, i.e. the second element in each of the elements in `obstacles`. It should return the re-calculated position back to the calling function. If none of the obstacles matched, it should simply return the position it had been given without making any changes.

The pseudo code for this function looks like this.

PseudoCode 6.6 Check for Obstacles

Require: *position*, *obstacles*

procedure CHECK FOR OBSTACLES
    for each obstacle in *obstacles* **do**
        if the first item in *obstacles* = *position* **then**
            position = *position*+ the second item in *obstacles*
        end if
    end for
    return *position*
end procedure

The code follows the pseudo code exactly.

Listing 6.4: Check for Obstacles

```
def checkForObstacles(position, obstacles):
    for obstacle in obstacles:
        if int(obstacle[0]) == position:
            position = position + int(obstacle[1])

    return position
```

You may have noticed that we're having to convert the element values into integers. That's because when we used the `csv` library to load the numbers, it treated them as strings, i.e. '13' rather than the number 13. Since `position` is an integer, we'll need to convert the first element to an integer before doing the comparison. Similarly, we need to convert the second element, i.e. the value that we're going to adjust the player's position by to an integer before adding it to `position`.

The code to play and handle obstacles is shown below. Notice that we've added an additional parameter, i.e. `obstacles` to `turn` which is then passed to `checkForObstacles`.

Listing 6.5: Code with obstacles but no grid (codeWithoutGrid.py)

```
import random
import csv

def loadObstacles():
# start by trying to load our data file.
  try:
    f = open("obstacles.csv", "r")

  except IOError as e:
    return []

  else:
    print("Obstacles file opened successfully")
    obstacles = []
    for line in csv.reader(f):
      obstacles.append(line)
    f.close()
    return obstacles

def throwDice(player):
    d1 = random.randint(1,6)
    d2 = random.randint(1,6)
    #d1 = int(input("First dice: "))
    #d2 = int(input("Second dice: "))

    if d1 == d2:
        score = -(d1+d2)
        print (player + ': double ' + str(d1) + ': returns ' + str(score))
```

```
    else:
        score = d1+d2
        print (player +' ' +str(d1) + ',' +str(d2) +': returns ' +str(score))
    return score

def checkForObstacles(position, player, obstacles):
    for obstacle in obstacles:
        if int(obstacle[0]) == position:
            print (player +": obstacle @ " +str(position) +", value " + obstacle[1]
            return position + int(obstacle[1])
    return position

def turn(position, player, obstacles):
    position = position + throwDice(player)
    position = checkForObstacles(position, player, obstacles)
    if position < 1:
        position = 1
    return position

def winner(position):
    if position > 48:
        return True
    else:
        return False


# program starts here
# Players A and B both start in square 1
A = 1
B = 1

obstacles = loadObstacles()
print(obstacles)

while True:
    A = turn(A, "A", obstacles)
    if winner(A):
        print ('Player A scored ' + str(A) + ', Player A has won')
        break
    else:
        print ('Player A new position: ' + str(A))
        B = turn(B, "B", obstacles)
        if winner(B):
            print ('Player B scored ' + str(B) + ', Player B has won')
            break
        else:
            print ('Player B new position: ' + str(B))
```

When we ran this we got the following trace and if you follow it through carefully you should be able to see exactly what is going on.

Program Output

```
Obstacles file opened successfully
[['12', '-2'], ['17', '3'], ['25', '7'], ['33', '-6'], ['39', '3']]
A 3,4: returns 7
Player A new position: 8
B: double 6: returns -12
Player B new position: 1
A 5,6: returns 11
Player A new position: 19
B 1,4: returns 5
Player B new position: 6
A 3,4: returns 7
Player A new position: 26
B 3,6: returns 9
Player B new position: 15
A 3,1: returns 4
Player A new position: 30
B 4,3: returns 7
Player B new position: 22
A 4,5: returns 9
A: obstacle @ 39, value 3
Player A new position: 42
B 6,4: returns 10
Player B new position: 32
A 5,4: returns 9
Player A scored 51, Player A has won
```

6.3 Messages

Apart from the graphics we've almost finished now. We've been asked to use an external file that's going to hold the messages that we're going to display. We've included quite a few to keep us in touch with what's going on. Rather than having them *hard coded* into the program it does make sense to keep them in a separate messages file. The reasons for this are twofold. By putting the messages inside a separate external file this means that we could easily replace them with messages in another language without changing the code. If for example we wrote our messages in French rather than English, all of the information that we displayed during the running of the program would then be in French. We wouldn't have to go trawling through our source code looking for messages to translate - everything would be in the single file that got loaded at startup. The second reason is less important, but by putting messages into an external file we're avoiding duplication. For example we might at various points in our code display the same message. By putting the messages into a separate file we can point to the same message, so we'll edit it in only one place - i.e. the external file. Avoiding duplication wherever possible is an important principle of programming design.

How we replace our current messages with messages brought in from an external file is quite simple. We'll open a new text file and copy and paste each of the messages dotted around our source code into the text file, putting each message on a separate line. We'll write some code to load the file and all of it's text into a `list`. Each item in the list will be a single message. If we, for sake of simplicity, call our list `m` then `m[0]` will give us the first message, `m[1]` the second and so on. We'll replace each of the text messages in our source file with the appropriate value of `m[N]` and we'll be good to go. Tedious but straightforward.

The pseudo code for the **`loadMessages`** function is very similar to the code we used to load the obstacles file. We'll first try to open the file. If we fail we'll return an empty list otherwise we'll create an empty list and then read the file into a list in one big gulp. We're not dealing with a comma separated file so we'll use a different Python function **`read().splitlines()`** which will read all the data, splitting each line neatly into a separate item in our list.

PseudoCode 6.7 Load Messages

```
procedure LOAD MESSAGES
    Try to open our messages file
    if this fails then
        return an empty list
    else
        Create an empty list called m
        Read the file into m
        Close the file
        return m
    end if
end procedure
```

The short program code to check that we've done this correctly is shown below.

Listing 6.6: Load messages file (loadMessages.py)

```
def loadMessages():
# start by trying to load our data file.
  try:
    f = open("messages.data", "r")

  except IOError as e:
    return None

  else:
    m = f.read().splitlines()
    f.close()
    return m

```

```
# program starts here
m = loadMessages()
print(m)
```

Those of you have worked your way through the book from the beginning might have noticed that we wrote our print statements a little differently in this problem. We've written lines such as the following.

```
print (player + ': double ' + str(d1) + ': returns ' + str(score))
```

This will print out something like

```
A: double 3: returns -6
```

We've concatenated a series of strings together to make up the final message, taking care to convert each integer value into a string before concatenating it. This is fine, but this way of writing print statements means that we'd need a string for ":double " and another for ":returns ". Let's suppose that m[13] was ":double " and m[14] was "returns ". We'd change our code to reflect this and we'd write the following instead.

```
print (player + m[13] + str(d1) + m[14] + str(score))
```

When we loaded our messages file, m[13] would be replaced by ":double " and m[14] by ""returns ". This works but it would be much better to rewrite our print statements like this instead.

```
print("%s: double %s: returns %s", %(player, str(d1), str(score)))
```

If you've been making your way through the book covering each problem in order you'd have already come across this way of writing print statements where the parameters to print are marked by the %s and are replaced in order by the contents of the brackets that follow.

If we use this technique we now only have a single message, say m[12] and we'd write the following.

```
print(m[12], %(player, str(d1), str(score)))
```

We've re-factored the last largish program we wrote (codeWithoutGrid.py), i.e. listing 6.5 on page 115 to take messages into account and the new version is shown below.

Listing 6.7: Code without Grid but with messages (codeWithoutGridMessages.py)

```
import random
import csv

def loadObstacles(m):
# start by trying to load our data file.
  try:
```

```
    f = open("obstacles.csv", "r")

  except IOError as e:
    return []

  else:
    print(m[2])
    obstacles = []
    for line in csv.reader(f):
      obstacles.append(line)
    f.close()
    return obstacles

def loadMessages():
# start by trying to load our data file.
  try:
    f = open("messages.data", "r")

  except IOError as e:
    return []

  else:
    m = f.read().splitlines()
    f.close()
    return m

def throwDice(player, m):
  d1 = random.randint(1,6)
  d2 = random.randint(1,6)
  #d1 = int(input("First dice: "))
  #d2 = int(input("Second dice: "))

  if d1 == d2:
    score = -(d1+d2)
    print (m[7] %(player, str(d1), str(score)))
  else:
    score = d1+d2
    print (m[8] %(player, str(d1), str(d2), str(score)))
  return score

def checkForObstacles(position, player, obstacles, m):
  for obstacle in obstacles:
    if int(obstacle[0]) == position:
      print(m[9] %(player, str(position), obstacle[1]))
      return position + int(obstacle[1])
  return position

def turn(position, player, obstacles, m):
  position = position + throwDice(player, m)
```

```
  position = checkForObstacles(position, player, obstacles, m)
  if position < 1:
    position = 1
  return position

def winner(position):
  if position > 48:
    return True
  else:
    return False


# program starts here
# Players A and B both start in square 1
A = 1
B = 1

m = loadMessages()
print(m[0])
print(m[1]) # welcome message
obstacles = loadObstacles(m)
print(obstacles)


while True:
  A = turn(A, "A", obstacles, m)
  if winner(A):
    print (m[3] %str(A))
    break
  else:
    print (m[4] %str(A))
    B = turn(B, "B", obstacles, m)
    if winner(B):
      print (m[5] %str(B))
      break
    else:
      print (m[6] % str(B))
```

The messages file that we created now looks like this.

```
Messages file loaded successfully
Welcome to our game
Obstacles file opened successfully
Player A scored %s, Player A has won
Player A new position: %s
Player B scored %s, Player B has won
Player B new position: %s
%s: double %s: returns %s
%s %s,%s returns %s
```

```
%s: obstacle @ %s, value %s
```

Running the program with this messages file on our system produces the following output. If you run the same code and messages file on your system you'll almost certainly get a different series of moves since your random generator won't produce the same die values. But the functionality should be identical.

Program Output

```
Messages file loaded successfully
Welcome to our game
Obstacles file opened successfully
[['12', '-2'], ['17', '3'], ['25', '7'], ['33', '-6'], ['39', '3']]
A: double 5: returns -10
Player A new position: 1
B 1,4 returns 5
Player B new position: 6
A 5,3 returns 8
Player A new position: 9
B 3,4 returns 7
Player B new position: 13
A 5,2 returns 7
Player A new position: 16
B 2,6 returns 8
Player B new position: 21
A 4,3 returns 7
Player A new position: 23
B 2,3 returns 5
Player B new position: 26
A 6,4 returns 10
A: obstacle @ 33, value -6
Player A new position: 27
B 2,6 returns 8
Player B new position: 34
A 3,4 returns 7
Player A new position: 34
B: double 1: returns -2
Player B new position: 32
A 3,2 returns 5
A: obstacle @ 39, value 3
Player A new position: 42
B 4,1 returns 5
Player B new position: 37
A: double 5: returns -10
Player A new position: 32
B 4,1 returns 5
Player B new position: 42
A: double 6: returns -12
Player A new position: 20
B 1,2 returns 3
```

```
Player B new position: 45
A 3,4 returns 7
Player A new position: 27
B 6,3 returns 9
Player B scored 54, Player B has won
```

We've now got a fully working program with the correct game play that we're asked to produce. Our obstacles are in an external file, our messages are in an external file and our simulated dice version is fully tested and working. It's a simple matter of changing two lines of code in `throwDice` to ask players for dice throws rather than simulating them, so what's left?

6.4 Graphics

Many of you might have wondered why, if we've been asked to display everything on a grid, we didn't start there. The reason is pretty simple. Concentrating on graphics from the beginning would have distracted us from the game play and this program is really all about the game play. In a very interesting sense, there is no need for a grid. A grid would suggest two dimensionality and our game is very much one dimensional. The positions of both of our players simply move through the integers starting at 1 according to the throw of two dice and with the help or hindrance of obstacles. There's no movement left or right, or even up and down as a grid would suggest.

Question: so what's the point of a grid?

Answer: To make it look pretty.

In addition, the grid complicates things quite a bit. We're going to have to draw the grid, we've got to put numbers on it that snake around the grid rather than always reading from left to right and we've got to show the position of each of our players on the grid as they move. We'll want to show some messages, presumably somewhere on the screen close to or alongside the grid itself and all the while our game play has to be correct.

Many students will have started this project by drawing the grid first and trying to write the game play directly using the grid. In our experience, this approach tends to get bogged down pretty quickly with matters that aren't actually very important. The game is perfectly playable without a grid and we've done that quite quickly with the code that we've already written. It's taken us quite a long time to write about what we did here, but the actual coding time was somewhat less than an hour in real time. You've got 20 hours to get the entire project analysed, designed, implemented, tested and evaluated which isn't a lot of time. The less time that you spend actually coding the better. This means adopting the approach that will give you the quickest way through the development and testing part. Simulating, rather than throwing actual dice speeds up development enormously, concentrating on the game play rather than worrying about the graphics is another.

With all of that said, we still have to produce a grid.

Let's start by looking at what we need to do. Pseudo code is a good way of organising our thoughts.

PseudoCode 6.8 Grid Requirements

```
Draw grid lines
Draw grid numbers
while no player has won do
    for each player do
        Calculate new position
        Update the grid
    end for
end while
Display a message saying who has won
```

We're going to leave aside our previous code for the moment. We'll start by writing some code to draw the lines of a grid and once that is working we'll write a function that given any integer N between 1 and 49 will tell us which square N should go on. This isn't quite as simple as it sounds because the task wants the numbers to 'snake' their way up the grid.

We have various choices for drawing graphics using Python. There's `pygame` which is *a cross platform set of Python modules designed for writing video games*. This is perhaps the most popular graphics system for Python, but there are dozens more. All we want to do is to draw a grid, some numbers and some way of showing the position of each player which suggests that something simple, quick and easy to program will be fine. Ideally, it should also be part of the standard python distribution so that we don't have to download anything special. With that in mind, the library `turtle`, documentation for which can be found at `https://docs.python.org/3/library/turtle.html` is a good bet. It draws lines, fills shapes with colour, has a drawing window on which you can put text and it's neat and simple. You may be familiar with other graphic system but we're sure that you'll find turtle graphics pretty neat once you try it. For these reasons, this is what we're going to use for our grid drawing program.

We'll start by writing code to create a window and we'll draw a square in the centre of the screen.

Turtle graphics is based on work done by Seymour Papert and Marvin Minsky at MIT in the USA decades ago. The principle is simple. You have a turtle that you can move around a screen by telling it to go forwards, backwards, turn by a given number of degrees. You can get it to draw in a colour of your choosing by picking a pen colour and telling it to put its pen down. You can move it without drawing by telling it to take its pen up and jumping to a given `(x,y)` coordinate. You can set background colours, fill shapes and so on. All of this is documented online and is available inside python by typing `import turtle` inside the python interpreter and then typing `dir(turtle)`. This gives you a list of all of the functions available to you. To get more information on any of the functions, for example **penup**, simply type **help(turtle.penup)**.

Programs are all about writing functions which call functions ...which call functions which do something. Turtle graphics are no different and its wise to take a very modular approach as you'll see as we progress to making our grid.

To create a window and to draw a square in the centre we can write the following.

Listing 6.8: Window and square (windowAndSquare.py)

```
import turtle

SLOW = 1


def jumpto(x,y):
    turtle.penup()
    turtle.goto(x,y)

def initialiseScreenAndTurtle():
    screen = turtle.Screen()
    screen.reset
    screen.setworldcoordinates(0, 0, 300, 300)
    turtle.title("A square")
    turtle.speed(SLOW)

def closeDown():
    turtle.done()

def square(side):
    turtle.pencolor("red")
    turtle.pendown()
    for _ in range(4):
        turtle.forward(side)
        turtle.right(90)


# program starts here
initialiseScreenAndTurtle()
jumpto(100,200)
square(100)
closeDown()
```

We've set the speed of drawing to be as slow as possible so that you can see exactly what is happening. If you look at the documentation for the **turtle.speed** function you'll see that a value of 0 makes it run as fast as possible, 1 is as slow as possible and numbers from 1 – 10 result in increasingly fast response. We've set the size of the drawing screen to be 300 x 300 and we've drawn a square of size 100 x 100 in red. That should all be pretty explanatory. We're not going to concentrate on the particular functions available in the turtle library - you'll be able to read about those yourselves, we'll simply get on with writing code to draw a grid.

Important note: position (0,0) is the bottom left hand corner of the window.

To draw a grid we'll need to.

- Initialise the turtle screen
- Leave space at the bottom of the screen for messages
- Draw a grid of 7 x 7 small squares
- Use constants as much as possible rather than numbers

Turtle graphics is all about co-ordinates so we took some graph paper to make a simple sketch showing where everything should be on the turtle screen. We'd like to position the grid neatly inside the window so we'd like to have the same space on the left of the grid as on the right and ideally above as well. We'll leave space for messages in the window area underneath the grid and we'll try to make our boxes look pretty square. Screen resolutions, e.g. 1024x768 are in the ration 4:3 so to make the boxes look square we're going to have the width of each square somewhat larger than the height and we'll make the window large enough to hold 49 squares with space around.

Here's some code to draw a grid following all of the points above. Again we've chosen the smallest drawing speed so that you can see exactly how the grid is drawn. We can of course speed this up any time we choose.

Listing 6.9: Draw a Grid (drawGrid.py)

```
import turtle

# grid origin lies at (10, 40)
OX = 10
OY = 40

# each cell (box) has dimensions (30,40) to make it look square
BOX_X = 30
BOX_Y = 40

#-------------------------------------
# Turtle graphics code
#-------------------------------------
def jumpto(x,y):
    turtle.penup()
    turtle.goto(x,y)

def line(x1, y1, x2, y2):
    jumpto(x1, y1)
    turtle.pendown()
```

```
    turtle.goto(x2, y2)
    turtle.penup()

def initialiseScreenAndTurtle():
    screen = turtle.Screen()
    screen.reset
    screen.setworldcoordinates(0, 0, OX + 8*BOX_X - 20, OY + 8*BOX_Y - 20)
    turtle.mode("world")
    turtle.speed(3)

def drawGrid():
    turtle.color('black')
    turtle.pensize(2)
    jumpto(OX, OY)
    for i in range(0,8):
        line(OX, i*BOX_Y + OY, OX + 7*BOX_X, i*BOX_Y + OY)
        line(i*BOX_X + OX, OY, i*BOX_X + OX, 7*BOX_Y + OY)

def closeDown():
    turtle.done()


# program starts here
initialiseScreenAndTurtle()
drawGrid()
closeDown()
```

if you run this code you'll see that we've used constants `OX` and `OY` to define the bottom left hand corner of our grid at `(10,40)`. We've set the y coordinate to 40 to make sure that we have room underneath for our messages. We've set our box (cell) size to 30 x 40 pixels to try to make the grid look reasonably square. We've set the screen size large enough to enclose the full size 7 x 7 grid with a little left over on the top and the sides to make it pretty central.

Essentially the turtle draws a series of horizontal lines starting from the left hand corner and moving up the y-axis in increments of `BOX_Y`, i.e. 40 pixels at a time. Interspersed between each horizontal drawing is a vertical drawing as the turtle moves along the x-axis `BOX_X`, i.e. 30 pixels at a time. The joint effect is to draw horizontally, vertically moving the start of the drawing position along both the y and x axes in turn until the full grid is drawn. The grid is drawn in black using a pen size of 2. That's it.

One point before we continue. We could have written `from turtle import *` which would mean that we didn't need to put `turtle.` before every turtle function call. We haven't done that specifically because we want you to see which calls are coming from the turtle library. It also means that if you wrote a **`penup`** function for example it wouldn't conflict with the `turtle.penup` function from the library. This might seem like a small point but it helps by making it very clear exactly where every function can be found, in your code or in a library that's been imported.

Now we want to move on to place the numbers in the centre of each of the cells (boxes) of the grid. Each box has dimensions 30 x 40 and it would be very useful to know which box each number should go into. If everything was on a straight line it would be simple. The number 1 would go into the first box, 2 would go into the second, 23 would go into the twenty third and so on. Our grid is more complicated. The bottom seven boxes reading from left to right will hold the numbers 1–7 but the next row up takes the numbers 14–8 and so on up the grid.

If we think of the grid as consisting of a series of rows and columns starting in the bottom left hand corner, the number 1 goes into row 0, column 0, 2 goes into row 0 column 1 and so on. With this naming convention, 43 for example will be row 6, column 0. The reason for thinking in rows and columns is that if we can find a simple formula that will convert any given number into the correct row and column pair we'll be able to place each number (and later each player's turtle) into the correct box. This is because it's easy to work out exactly what pixel is at the bottom left hand corner of any box given its row and column pair.

To show you what we mean, suppose by looking at the grid I can see that 26 is in row 3 and column 2 (counting always starts at zero). What are the x and y pixel values of the bottom left hand corner of that box? Well, if each box is 30 pixels wide and 40 pixels high and if the bottom left hand corner of our grid, i.e. the origin is at (10,40) then to find the x coordinate of our box we simply multiply the width of each box (30) by the number of columns, i.e. 2 and add the x value of our origin, i.e. 10 to it giving us 70. Similarly by multiplying the number of rows by the height of each row and adding the value of the y coordinate of the origin we get 160. This means that the number 26 has to go in the middle of the box whose bottom left coordinate pair is (70,160). To make sure that we're writing the number into roughly the centre of the box we'll add a few pixels onto both the x and the y values.

Hopefully that's clear. If not, grab a cup of coffee, put your feet up and read it again slowly with a pen and paper in your hand to make a simple drawing of what's going on.

Continuing. If we know the row and column that a particular number needs to go into we'll be able to position the numbers correctly and also each player. It's important to realise that each player is going to move along the board too. At any given moment, each player's position is simply a number in the range 0–49 so to draw each player onto the board we're going to need to know which box to draw them in. As you'll see shortly, we're going to draw a red turtle in the top left hand corner of the box for one player and a blue turtle in the top right hand corner for the other. Both will be drawn so as not to obscure the number in the centre of the box. This means that knowing which box to draw them in is crucial. This means that it is really important to translate any given n in the range 1–49 into the correct row and column combination. The $64,000,000 question is how to do this.

6.5 Converting n to (row, column)

The grid, shown in 6.1, is drawn again below in Table 6.2. If you look closely at the pattern of numbers you can immediately see that counting row 0 as the bottom row and row 6 as the top row, rows 0, 2, 4 and 6 all have the numbers increasing from left to right whereas tows 1, 3 and 5 have the numbers decreasing from left to right. In simple terms, the even numbered rows (assuming 0 is even) have increasing numbers, the odd rows have decreasing numbers. You might also notice something quite neat. For any given number n, if we take one away from it and then perform an integer divide of 7 we get 0 for all the numbers in the bottom row, (i.e. row 0), 1 for all numbers in the next row, (i.e. row 1), 2 for all numbers in row 2 and so on. This means that to find what row any given number n is on, all we have to do is perform the calculation `(n-1) // 7` and the resulting value is the correct row.

So far so good. How about the column?

If the row is even, take 1 from the number and find the remainder when divided by 7. In python this is simply `(n-1) % 7`. Try it and you'll see it works, but only if the row is even.

What if the row is odd? Do exactly the same calculation as if the row was even but take the result away from 6, i.e. `6 - ((n-1) %7)`. Try it.

How do we know if a row is even? We simply have to see whether the remainder, i.e. the modulus if it's divided by 2 is zero. If it is, it's even otherwise it is odd.

Examples:

The number 23 is on row $(23 - 1)//7$ which is $22//7 = 3$. Is this an even row? i.e. Is $3\%7 = 0$? No, so it's an odd row. Which column? Answer, $6 - (23 - 1)\%7 = 5$. So 23 is in the box 3 rows up, 5 columns across (counting from 0).

The number 31 is on row $(31-1)//7$ which is $30//7 = 4$. Is this even? i.e. Is $4\%7 = 0$? Yes, so it's an even row. Which column? Answer. $(31 - 1)\%7 = 2$. So 31 is in box 4 rows up, 2 columns across counting from 0.

43	44	45	46	47	48	49
42	41	40	39	38	37	36
29	30	31	32	33	34	35
28	27	26	25	24	23	22
15	16	17	18	19	20	21
14	13	12	11	10	9	8
1	2	3	4	5	6	7

Table 6.2: The board

With all of that said, here's some pseudo code for our function to convert any integer n in the range 1–49 to its row and column combination.

PseudoCode 6.9 Convert N

Require: n

```
procedure CONVERT N
    row = (n − 1)//7
    if row is even then
        column = (n − 1)%7
    else
        column = 6 − ((n − 1)%7)
    end if
    return row, column
end procedure
```

Some code to print out the column and row combinations for the integers 1–49 is as follows so that we can check that we've thought this through correctly is as follows.

Listing 6.10: Row and column (rowAndColumn.py)

```
def getColRowFor(n):
  row = (n-1) // 7
  if (row % 2) == 0: # i.e. numbers increase from left to right
    col = (n-1) % 7
  else: # numbers decrease from left to right
    col = (7 - (n%7)) % 7

  return col, row

def printNColRow():
  for n in range (1,50):
    col, row = getColRowFor(n)
    print (str(n) + ': (' + str(row) + ', ' + str(col) + ')')

# program begins here
printNColRow()
```

The output from running this is (somewhat truncated).

Program Output

```
1: (0, 0)
2: (0, 1)
3: (0, 2)
4: (0, 3)
5: (0, 4)
6: (0, 5)
7: (0, 6)
```

```
8: (1, 6)
...
43: (6, 0)
44: (6, 1)
45: (6, 2)
46: (6, 3)
47: (6, 4)
48: (6, 5)
49: (6, 6)
```

Now that we've got a nice function that given any arbitrary n in the range 1–49 will give us the correct row and column combination, we can write a program to print both the grid and to position each number in the centre of its correct box. We need an additional function which we'll call **drawN** which when given a number n and the column and row values will write n in the middle of the correct box. **drawN** uses the function **turtle.write()** which takes 4 parameters, (1) the string to write, (2) True - meaning move the pen to the bottom right hand corner of the text, (3) alignment and (4) what font to use. The code is shown below.

Listing 6.11: Grid with numbers (numbers.py)

```
import turtle

# grid origin lies at (10, 40)
OX = 10
OY = 40

# box has dimensions (30,40) to make it look square
BOX_X = 30
BOX_Y = 40

# turtle drawing speed
SUPERFAST = 0

#-------------------------------------
# Turtle graphics code
#-------------------------------------
def jumpto(x,y):
    turtle.penup()
    turtle.goto(x,y)

def line(x1, y1, x2, y2):
    jumpto(x1, y1)
    turtle.pendown()
    turtle.goto(x2, y2)
    turtle.penup()

def initialiseScreenAndTurtle():
```

```
    screen = turtle.Screen()
    screen.reset
    screen.setworldcoordinates(0, 0, OX + 8*BOX_X -20, OY + 8*BOX_Y - 20)
    turtle.mode("world")
    turtle.hideturtle()
    turtle.speed(SUPERFAST)

def drawGrid():
    turtle.color('black')
    turtle.pensize(2)
    jumpto(OX, OY)
    for i in range(0,8):
        line(OX, i*BOX_Y + OY, OX + 7*BOX_X, i*BOX_Y + OY)
        line(i*BOX_X + OX, OY, i*BOX_X + OX, 7*BOX_Y + OY)

def drawN(n, col, row):
    jumpto(OX + col*BOX_X+10, OY + row*BOX_Y+10)
    turtle.write(str(n), True, align="left", font = ("Arial", 28, "normal"))

def getColRowFor(n):
    row = (n-1) // 7
    if (row % 2) == 0: # i.e. numbers increase from left to right
        col = (n-1) % 7
    else: # numbers decrease from left to right
        col = 6 - ((n-1) % 7)

    return col, row

def drawNumbers():
    for n in range (1,50):
        col, row = getColRowFor(n)
        drawN(n, col, row)

def closeDown():
    turtle.done()


# program starts here
initialiseScreenAndTurtle()
drawGrid()
drawNumbers()
closeDown()
```

We're now getting pretty close to finishing the code. We've already written the game play code, we've drawn a grid, we've positioned the numbers in the centre of the grid. All we have left to do now is to integrate the game play with the graphics code, add a little drawing code to position each player after they've moved using the same function as we've used to place the numbers and we'll have finished.

Let's look at the original game play code as shown in listing 6.7 and have a think about what we need to do to integrate the code as quickly and as cleanly as possible.

Using our new graphics code we want to show where each player is at any given time. We have two players, player A and player B. The position of player A at any time is given by the variable `A` while the position of player B at any time is given by the variable `B`. In the main body of the program, once player A has has had his turn, we check to see if player A has won. If so, we print a message to say so and we exit. If not, we print an appropriate message and move on to give player B a turn. In either case, calling function `turn` gives us a new position for a player. This would be the most appropriate time to draw the player's new position on the board.

Additionally, it would be nice to put out exactly the same messages as we've been showing for the non grid version. We could print them to the screen as we have done before but we've left room for messages on the same window as the grid so it makes sense to make use of the space. To do so we'll need a new function, let's call it `message` that is given a string to display on the board. Everywhere we currently call `print`, we'll simply use `message`. The transition should be seamless.

One little sticking point with `message` is that since we're going to display every message in the same place, we'd better get rid of the previous message otherwise we'll simply end up with an awful mess on the screen. This suggests that to show messages we simply

- Clear our drawing area
- Write a message in our drawing area

Simply writing a line of empty text won't clear the line. The background colour for our window by default is white so to clear the text area we're going to have to draw a rectangle that's large enough to cover our text area. We'll fill the rectangle with white which will get rid of any text. The code for the two functions is shown below.

Listing 6.12: Text box for messages (textbox.py)

```
# messages start at (10,10)
MSG_X = 10
MSG_Y = 10

#-----------------------------------
def clearMessageLine():
    jumpto(MSG_X-2, MSG_Y)
    turtle.setheading(90)
    turtle.fillcolor("white")
    turtle.begin_fill()
    for _ in range(2):
        turtle.forward(10)
        turtle.right(90)
        turtle.forward(280)
        turtle.right(90)
```

```
    turtle.end_fill()

#-----------------------------------
def message(msg):
    clearMessageLine()
    jumpto(MSG_X, MSG_Y)
    turtle.pencolor("black")
    turtle.write(msg, True, align="left", font = ("Arial", 16, "normal"))
```

As you can see from the code, we'll pass a string called `msg` into `message`. The first thing `message` does is to call `clearMessageLine` which uses the turtle drawing functions to draw and fill a rectangle with white. Once it's done that we return to `messsage` which jumps back to the start of the line, sets the pen colour to black and writes whatever text it's been given. Note that we're using the two constants `MSG_X` and `MSG_Y` to keep track of the left hand corner of our text drawing area. This is useful because if we wanted to put the text area anywhere else, all we'd have to do is to change the values of these two constants and run again. We wouldn't have to change anything else in the code. Hence the value of constants. As mentioned previously, python doesn't really have constants but other languages do and its conventional to put them in upper case letters. We're not changing them in the body of the code so we're treating them as constants.

So that's messages taken care of. Finally, let's see what we need to do to draw our players on the grid.

We've got the extremely useful function `getColRowFor` which translates any n to a corresponding row, column combination which we can use to find the bottom left hand corner of the box that our player needs to be shown in. The turtle itself is a pretty little arrow which we can colour as we like. If we select red for player A, blue for player B and agree that we'll put A in the top left hand corner of the box and B in the top right hand corner of the box, then if both players happen to land on the same value they won't overwrite each other and we'll be able to see it. One small niggle is that we'll need to remove the position each player was previously when we draw the new position. Turtle graphics has a function `turtle.stamp()` which returns a `stamp_ID`, presumably an integer but we don't really need to know. All we need to do is to keep track of the `stamp_ID` for each player and when it's their turn to get displayed we should clear the previous stamp before stamping at the new position. With these comments in mind, the final code for both real and simulated versions of the game with full graphics support are as follows.

Listing 6.13: Complete code - Sample 3 (sample3.py)

```
import random
import turtle
import csv

# grid origin lies at (10, 40)
OX = 10
OY = 40

```

```
# messages go to (10,10)
MSG_X = 10
MSG_Y = 10

# box has dimensions (30,40) to make it look square
BOX_X = 30
BOX_Y = 40

# turtle speed
NORMAL = 8
SLOW = 3
FAST = 5
SUPERFAST = 0

# real dice or SIMULATION
# change this flag to False to produce a real dice version of this program
SIMULATION = True

#-------------------------------------
# Turtle graphics code
#-------------------------------------
def jumpto(x,y):
  turtle.penup()
  turtle.goto(x,y)

#-------------------------------------
def line(x1, y1, x2, y2):
  jumpto(x1, y1)
  turtle.pendown()
  turtle.goto(x2, y2)
  turtle.penup()

#-------------------------------------
def clearMessageLine():
  jumpto(MSG_X-2, MSG_Y-2)
  turtle.setheading(90)
  turtle.fillcolor("white")
  turtle.begin_fill()
  for _ in range(2):
    turtle.forward(12)
    turtle.right(90)
    turtle.forward(280)
    turtle.right(90)
    turtle.end_fill()

#-------------------------------------
def message(msg):
  clearMessageLine()
  jumpto(MSG_X, MSG_Y)
```

```
  turtle.pencolor("black")
  turtle.write(msg, True, align="left", font = ("Arial", 16, "normal"))

#-------------------------------------
def drawGrid():
  turtle.color('black')
  turtle.pensize(2)
  jumpto(OX, OY)
  for i in range(0,8):
    line(OX, i*BOX_Y + OY, OX + 7*BOX_X, i*BOX_Y + OY)
    line(i*BOX_X + OX, OY, i*BOX_X + OX, 7*BOX_Y + OY)

#-------------------------------------
def initialiseScreenAndTurtle():
  screen = turtle.Screen()
  screen.reset
  screen.setworldcoordinates(0, 0, OX + 8*BOX_X - 20, OY + 8*BOX_Y - 20)
  turtle.title("Sample 3 - Game of dice")
  turtle.mode("world")
  turtle.hideturtle()
  turtle.speed(SUPERFAST)

#-------------------------------------
def drawN(n, col, row):
  jumpto(OX + col*BOX_X+10, OY + row*BOX_Y+10)
  turtle.write(str(n), True, align="left", font = ("Arial", 28, "normal"))

#-------------------------------------
def getColRowFor(n):
  row = (n-1) // 7
  if (row % 2) == 0: # i.e. numbers increase from left to right
    col = (n-1) % 7
  else: # numbers decrease from left to right
    col = 6 - ((n-1) % 7)

  return col, row

#-------------------------------------
def drawNumbers():
  for n in range (1,50):
    col, row = getColRowFor(n)
    drawN(n, col, row)

#-------------------------------------
def drawPlayerAt(col, row, Player, stampID):
  turtle.clearstamp(stampID)
  if Player == "A":
    jumpto(OX + col*BOX_X+5, OY + row*BOX_Y + BOX_Y - 5)
    turtle.color("red")
```

```
    return turtle.stamp()
  else:
    jumpto(OX + col*BOX_X+BOX_X-5, OY + row*BOX_Y + BOX_Y - 5)
    turtle.color("blue")
    return turtle.stamp()

#------------------------------------
def showPlayerOnGrid(position, Player, stampID):
  col, row = getColRowFor(position)
  return drawPlayerAt(col, row, Player, stampID)

#------------------------------------
def closeDown():
  turtle.done()

#------------------------------------
# Gameplay code
#------------------------------------
def loadObstacles(m):
# start by trying to load our data file.
  try:
    f = open("obstacles.csv", "r")

  except IOError as e:
    return []

  else:
    message(m[2])
    obstacles = []
    for line in csv.reader(f):
      obstacles.append(line)
    f.close()
    return obstacles

#------------------------------------
def loadMessages():
# start by trying to load our data file.
  try:
    f = open("messages.data", "r")

  except IOError as e:
    return []

  else:
    m = f.read().splitlines()
    f.close()
    return m

#------------------------------------
```

```
def throwDice(player, m):
  if (SIMULATION):
    d1 = random.randint(1,6)
    d2 = random.randint(1,6)
  else:
    d1 = int(turtle.numinput(m[7] + Player, m[17], minval=1, maxval=6))
    d2 = int(turtle.numinput(m[7] + Player, m[18], minval=1, maxval=6))

  if d1 == d2:
    score = -(d1+d2)
    message (m[7] %(player, str(d1), str(score)))
  else:
    score = d1+d2
    message (m[8] %(player, str(d1), str(d2), str(score)))
  return score

#-------------------------------------
def checkForObstacles(position, player, obstacles, m):
  for obstacle in obstacles:
    if int(obstacle[0]) == position:
      message(m[9] %(player, str(position), obstacle[1]))
      return position + int(obstacle[1])
  return position

#-------------------------------------
def turn(position, player, obstacles, m):
  position = position + throwDice(player, m)
  position = checkForObstacles(position, player, obstacles, m)
  if position < 1:
    position = 1
  return position

#-------------------------------------
def winner(position):
  if position > 48:
    return True
  else:
    return False

#---------------------------------
# program starts here
initialiseScreenAndTurtle()
drawGrid()
drawNumbers()

# both players start on the first square of the grid
A = 1
B = 1
```

```
# having drawn the grid quickly we can slow down
turtle.speed(NORMAL)

# load messages and obstacles
m = loadMessages()
obstacles = loadObstacles(m)

# keep track of the last turtle position for each players
# so that we can delete in before showing the new position
stampA = None
stampB = None

# quick welcome message
message(m[1])

while True:
  if (SIMULATION):
    turtle.speed(FAST)

  A = turn(A, "A", obstacles, m)
  if winner(A):
    message (m[3] %str(A))
    stampA = showPlayerOnGrid(49, "A", stampA)
    break
  else:
    message (m[4] %str(A))
    stampA = showPlayerOnGrid(A, "A", stampA)

  if (SIMULATION):
    turtle.speed(NORMAL)
    turtle.speed(FAST)

  B = turn(B, "B", obstacles, m)
  if winner(B):
    message (m[5] %str(B))
    stampB = showPlayerOnGrid(49, "B", stampB)
    break
  else:
    message (m[6] %str(B))
    stampB = showPlayerOnGrid(B, "B", stampB)

  if (SIMULATION):
    turtle.speed(NORMAL)

closeDown()
```

As you can see we've created a variable called `SIMULATION`[4] which is set to `True` at the

[4] We call this type of thing a flag. Americans call them semaphores, they simply take on `True` or `False` values

start of the code. This flag is used to select which code runs in the very small number of places where there is a difference between the simulated and real dice version of the game. Setting this flag to `False` will allow you to run the real dice version. The only places where the code differs are in the `throwDice` function where we actually get the dice values rather than simulating them and in the main body of the code where we've changed the turtle drawing speed a little to make the simulated version run neatly.

We mentioned using the `turtle.stamp()` function to keep track of the previous position of each player. As you can see from the code the values for the stamps of both players is passed from the main body of code through `showPlayerOnGrid` to `drawPlayerAt` where it is used to clear the previous stamp before stamping the player's new position. Note also the use of `getColRowFor` to return the row and column combination for where we want to position the player. These small but incredibly useful functions allow us to take the approach that we have.

For completeness, the messages file we've used is

Program Output

```
Messages file loaded successfully
Welcome to our game
Obstacles file opened successfully
Player A scored %s, Player A has won
Player A new position: %s
Player B scored %s, Player B has won
Player B new position: %s
%s: double %s: returns %s
%s %s,%s returns %s
%s: obstacle @ %s, value %s
```

The obstacles file is

Program Output

```
12,-2
17,3
25,7
33,-6
39,3
```

which are used to decide between two possibilities

7

Final thoughts

For those of you who have managed to get through all of the book, congratulations. It hasn't been an easy read I'm sure, but that's the nature of the beast I'm afraid. Programming is hard, it requires you to think possibly harder than you do in any other subject. Reading code is time consuming and you need to focus for extended periods of time. As Euclid once said to King Ptolemy I Soter,"There is no royal road to geometry" meaning that there was no shortcut. Exactly the same can be said for programming. The only way to improve is to write code. Hopefully books like this should help you, if only a little bit to think clearly about problems. Writing good code isn't necessarily about being clever, it's about being clear.

- Functions should be short, certainly no more than once screen page or one A4 page.
- Code should be self-documenting with good variable and function names.
- Use constants when variables never change.
- Data structures come first
- Doodle, draw pictures, write pseudo code.
- Code only when ready.
- Test constantly.
- Don't be afraid to change the design once you really understand the problem.
- Time spent writing utility functions pays for itself many times over, e.g. `displayList`.
- Keep external data in text files if at all possible.

Programmers often keep in mind the acronym KISS, i.e. Keep It Simple Stupid. Don't try to be too clever. The best solution is often the clearest not the cleverest.

Good luck with your projects.

Final thoughts

Appendices

A

File resources

All source files including those below can be downloaded from `https://github.com/BagatellePublications/GCSE-CompSci-Programming-Guide`. Select the green button (Clone or Download) on the right of the page and select the option 'Download ZIP' to save a complete copy of all source files to your computer.

students.csv

```
['23876','Parker','Peter','23-05-2003','34 Parkway,Oxford,OX2 OUD',
'01865325645','M','5LM','23876@treeroad.sch.uk']
['17893','Tomas','Tim','12-06-2003','15 The Oaks,Oxford,OX2 OTY','',
'M','5LM','17893@treeroad.sch.uk']
['21789','Smith','Versa','15-01-2003','12 John Street,Oxford,OX1 2TT',
'018652211145','F','5LM','21789@treeroad.sch.uk']
['91','Acha','Nero','17-04-2003','17 Peter Rd,Oxford,OX1 2AB',
'018652781142','M','5LM','91@treeroad.sch.uk']
['14356','Williams','Tom','25-09-2009','9 Acres Rd Oxford,OX2 2AY',
'07311228776','M','5LM','14356@treeroad.sch.uk']
['324','Patel','Aya','12-12-2002','3 London Rd,Oxford,OX3 2UI',
'01865457658','F','5LM','324@treeroad.sch.uk']
['17112','Mosel','Eva','19-08-2003','91 Magdalen Rd,Oxford,OX4 7GT',
'074122255645','F','5LM','17112@treeroad.sch.uk']
['4563','Pears','Anwen','19-03-2003','72 Court Close,Oxford,OX3 1HY',
'01865788445','F','5LM','4563@treeroad.sch.uk']
['2900','Preston','Elinor','09-04-2003',"65 Tom's way,Oxford,OX4 9UY",
'','F','5LM','2900@treeroad.sch.uk']
['11267','Bell','Mischa','01-12-2002','12 Maple Rd,Oxford,OX2 1FG',
'','F','5LM','11267@treeroad.sch.uk']
['22113','Long','Albert','17-03-2003','3 Tom Rd,Oxford,OX1 2AY',
'01865192837','M','5LM','22113@treeroad.sch.uk']
```

```
['321','Spoor','Evie','12-02-2003','8 Long Street,Oxford,OX1 2TT',
'01865668779','F','5LM','321@treeroad.sch.uk']
['78932','Smith','Mary','09-07-2003','47 Long Street,Oxford,OX1 2TU',
'01865156849','F','5LM','78932@treeroad.sch.uk']
['66733','Patel','Simla','','81 Boars Hill,Oxford,OX11 2TR',
'0186577899','F','5LM','66733@treeroad.sch.uk']
['2231','Owen','Trevor','18-05-2003','5 Marsh Lane,Oxford,OX3 2TY',
'0186520453','M','5LM','2231@treeroad.sch.uk']
['443','Gras','Ossie','13-04-2003','5 Bilge Street,Oxford,OX5 1GH',
'01865447855','M','5LM','443@treeroad.sch.uk']
['22978','Priest','May','11-11-2102','Dunroaming,Oxford,OX4 8DF',
'0186520017','F','5LM','22978@treeroad.sch.uk']
['1321','Toms','Lisa','15-09-2002','','','F','5LM',
'1321@treeroad.sch.uk']
['2238','Herbert','Liz','23-01-2003','9 Piggot Street,Oxford,OX4 2FG',
'','F','5LM','2238@treeroad.sch.uk']
['5542','Gras','Hannah','28-04-2003','','','F','5LM',
'5542@treeroad.sch.uk']
['4452','Hignam','Megan','29-05-2003','9 College Rd,Oxford,OX1 8HH',
'018659978545','F','5LM','4452@treeroad.sch.uk']
['3468','Toole','Peter','14-03-2003','15 Small Rd,Oxford,OX1 4HU',
'01865332665','M','5LM','3468@treeroad.sch.uk']
['967','Bora','Zarek','12-10-2002','9 Lupin Close,Oxford,OX4 4CV',
'01865334995','M','5LM','967@treeroad.sch.uk']
['67','Peters','Will','21-07-2003','','07523127865','M','5LM',
'67@treeroad.sch.uk']
['1123','Arbuthnott','Charlie','12-12-2001','46 London Rd,
Oxford,OX3 4HG','0123981723','M','5LM','1123@treeroad.sch.uk']
['2211','Peters','Mary','13-07-2002','43 New Road,Oxford,)X1 2TG',
'01283761827','','5LM','2211@treeroad.sch.uk']
['876876','Peters','Arnold','12-12-1956','2 Cornmarket,Oxford,OX3 1HG',
'01865 2232212','','5LM','876876@treeroad.sch.uk']
```

films.pkl (text)

```
['Avatar',['sci-fi','action'],['Sam Worthington','Sigourney Weaver',
'Zoe Saldana'],'James Cameron']
['Guardians of the Galaxy',['sci-fi','comedy'],['Chris Pratt',
'James Gunn','Vin Diesel','Zoe Saldana'],'James Gunn']
['Pirates of the Caribbean:The curse of the Black Pearl',['action',
'comedy'],['Johnny Depp','Orlando Bloom','Keira Knightley'],
'Gore Verbinski']
['Tootsie',['comedy'],['Dustin Hoffman','Jessica Lange','Bill Murray'],
'Sydney Pollack']
['The Godfather',['drama'],['Marlon Brando','Al Pacino','James Caan'],
'Francis Ford Coppola']
```

```
['A Woman Under the Influence',['drama'],['Gena Rowlans','Peter Falk',
'Fred Draper'],'John Cassavetes']
['Cinema Paradiso',['romantic'],['Philippe Noiret','Enzo Cannavale',
'Antonella Attili'],'Giuseppe Tornatore']
['To Kill a Mockingbird',['drama'],['Gregory Peck','John Megna',
'Frank Overton'],'Robert Mulligan']
['The Godfather: Part II',['drama'],['Al Pacino','Robert De Niro',
'Robert Duvall'],'Francis Ford Coppola']
['Annie Hall',['comedy','romance'],['Woody Allen','Diane Keaton'],
'Woody Allen']
['Boogie Nights',['comedy','drama'],['Mark Wahlberg','Julianne
Moore','Burt Reynolds'],'Paul Thomas Anderson']
['Taxi Driver',['drama'],['Robert De Niro','Jodie Foster','Cybill
Shepherd'],'Martin Scorsese']
['Dog Day Afternoon',['drama'],['Al Pacino','John Cazale',
'Penelope Allen'],'Sidney Lumet']
['Goodfellas',['drama'],['Robert De Niro','Ray Liotta','Joe Pesci'],
'Martin Scorsese']
['Withnail and I',['black comedy','indie'],['Richard E Grant','Paul
McGann','Richard Griffiths'],'Bruce Robinson']
['Kes',['drama'],['David Bradley','Brian Glover','Freddie Fletcher'],
'Ken Loach']
['The Wizard of Oz',['musical','fantasy','family'],['Judy Garland',
'Frank Morgan','Ray Bolger'],'Victor Fleming']
['On the Waterfront',['drama'],['Marlon Brando','Karl Madden',
'Lee J Cobb'],'Elia Kazan']
['The Shining',['horror'],['Jack Nicholson','Shelley Duval','Danny
Lloyd'],'Stanley Kubrick']
['Pulp Fiction',['thriller','black comedy','comedy','drama'],['John
Travolta','Uma Thurman','Samuel L Jackson'],'Quentin Tarantino']
['Gladiator',['action','drama'],['Russell Crowe','Joaquin Phoenix',
'Connie Nielsen'],'Ridley Scott']
['Jaws',['action','thriller','drama'],['Roy Scheider','Robert Shaw',
'Richard Dreyfuss'],'Steven Spielberg']
['Raging Bull',['drama','sports'],['Robert De Niro','Cathy Moriarty',
'Joe Pesci'],'Martin Scorcese']
["Who's afraid of Virginia Woolf",['black comedy','drama'],
['Elizabeth Taylor','Richard Burton','George Segal'],'Mike Nichols']
['Some Like It Hot',['comedy'],['Marilyn Monroe','Tony Curtis',
'Jack Lemmon'],'Billy Wilder']
['Fargo',['black comedy','drama'],['Frances McDormand','Steve
Buscemi','William H Macy'],'Joel Coen']
['The Night of The Hunter',['drama','thriller'],['Robert Mitchum',
'Shelley Wintera','Billy Chapin'],'Charles Laughton']
["Rosemary's Baby",['horror'],['Mia Farrow','John Cassavetes',
'Ruth Gordon'],'Roman Polanski']
```

```
['Chinatown',['thriller','drama'],['Jack Nicholson','Faye Dunaway',
'John Huston'],'Roman Polanski']
['The Apartment',['comedy'],['Jack Lemmon','Shirley MacLaine',
'Fred MacMurray'],'Billy Wilder']
```

customers.pkl (text)

```
['pwilliams','Password1','Peter Williams','26 High Street,
Kensington,SW10 3ET',"14-01-1993'",'M',['films','tv','music'],
[['Avatar',['sci-fi','action'],['Sam Worthington','Sigourney Weaver',
'Zoe Saldana'],'James Cameron','Y'],['Guardians of the Galaxy',
['sci-fi','comedy'],['Chris Pratt','James Gunn','Vin Diesel','Zoe
Saldana'],'James Gunn','Y'],['Fargo',['black comedy','drama'],
['Frances McDormand','Steve Buscemi','William H Macy'],'Joel
Coen','N']]]
['athos','P576swwd','Tom Sawyer','11 Trim Street,Kensington,
SW10 2TY','15-12-1987','M',['movies','running','squash'],
[['Taxi Driver',['drama'],['Robert De Niro','Jodie Foster','Cybill
Shepherd'],'Martin Scorsese','Y'],['The Wizard of Oz',['musical',
'fantasy','family'],['Judy Garland','Frank Morgan','Ray Bolger'],
'Victor Fleming','N'],['Some Like It Hot',['comedy'],['Marilyn
Monroe','Tony Curtis','Jack Lemmon'],'Billy Wilder','N']]]
```

obstacles.csv

```
12,-2
17,3
25,7
33,-6
39,3
```

messages.data

```
Messages file loaded successfully
Welcome to our game
Obstacles file opened successfully
Player A scored %s, Player A has won
Player A new position: %s
Player B scored %s, Player B has won
Player B new position: %s
%s: double %s: returns %s
%s %s,%s returns %s
%s: obstacle @ %s, value %s
```

Lightning Source UK Ltd.
Milton Keynes UK
UKHW021435041120
372791UK00007B/631

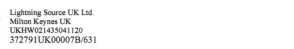

9 780957 140233